Creative Critical Interventions for Social Justice

COMPARATIVE LITERATURE AND CULTURE

Series Editors: Timothy Mathews and Florian Mussgnug

Comparative Literature and Culture explores new creative and critical perspectives on literature, art and culture. Contributions offer a comparative, cross-cultural and interdisciplinary focus, showcasing exploratory research in literary and cultural theory and history, material and visual cultures, and reception studies. The series is also interested in language-based research, particularly the changing role of national and minority languages and cultures, and includes within its publications the annual proceedings of the 'Hermes Consortium for Literary and Cultural Studies'.

Timothy Mathews is Emeritus Professor of French and Comparative Criticism, UCL.

Florian Mussgnug is Professor of Comparative Literature and Italian Studies, UCL.

Creative Critical Interventions for Social Justice

Edited by Natasha Tanna,
Abeyamí Ortega Domínguez and
Hakan Sandal-Wilson

UCLPRESS

First published in 2026 by
UCL Press
University College London
Gower Street
London WC1E 6BT

Available to download free: www.uclpress.co.uk

A CIP catalogue record for this book is available from the British Library.

ISBN: 978-1-80655-004-3 (Hbk)
ISBN: 978-1-80655-005-0 (Pbk)
ISBN: 978-1-80655-006-7 (PDF)
ISBN: 978-1-80655-007-4 (epub)
DOI: https://doi.org/10.14324/111.9781806550067

Contents

List of figures

List of contributors

Natasha Tanna is Senior Lecturer in World Literature in the Department of English and Related Literature, University of York. Prior to taking up her post at York she was Leverhulme Early Career Fellow in the Department of Spanish and Portuguese, UCL, and Lecturer in Spanish at the University of Cambridge. Her first monograph, *Queer Genealogies in Transnational Barcelona* (Legenda 2019) won the 2018 Publication Prize of the Association of Hispanists of Great Britain and Ireland. She specialises in contemporary literary engagements with queer theory, decolonial theory and critical race theory. Her areas of expertise include Latin(x) American and Caribbean literature, as well as Iberian literature in Spanish and Catalan.

Abeyamí Ortega Domínguez is Honorary Research Associate in Social Anthropology at the School of Social Sciences, University of Manchester. Her research explores how creative practices relate to the production and countering of social inequalities, from intersectional perspectives and anti-racist frameworks. She has conducted research on art and social justice, on racism and visuality, and on migration, embodied aesthetics and cultural heritage in transnational contexts. She has co-convened collaborative projects linking scholarly, activist and artistic work through creative methods in Latin and North America, Africa and Europe. She has taught at the University of Cambridge, at the National Autonomous University of Mexico and the National School of Anthropology of Mexico.

Hakan Sandal-Wilson is Assistant Professor of Gender, Peace and Security at the Department of Gender Studies at the LSE. Before joining the LSE, he was Teaching Associate in Sociology at Downing College, University of Cambridge, and an Affiliated Lecturer at the University of Cambridge Centre for Gender Studies. His research explored democracy, social movements and the intersections of ethnic, religious, gender and sexual identities in conflict-affected states and societies in the Middle East, with a particular focus on Kurdish LGBTI+ activism in Turkey. Hakan is invested in exploring and developing research methods and methodologies in conversation with creative writing and literature.

Princess Arinola Adegbite aka **P. A. Bitez** is an Afro-futurist writer, spoken-word poet, musician, actress and filmmaker from Manchester. Her work explores identity, technology and relationships. She is a winner of Slambassadors, BBC Words First 2020 and Slam-O-Vision 2021 finalist. Her awards include Manchester Creative of the Year 2021 and an Eric Gregory Award 2023 from the Society of Authors for her in progress collection *Algorithms of Meaning*. Bitez is an active member of the Writing Squad, and a Factory Sounds, Youth Music and Help Musicians funded musician. Bitez has been commissioned by Chanel, Selfridges, BBC, Ripples of Hope Festival, Elizabeth Gaskell House, British Triathlon and many more. Bitez's work is included in publications by Arachne Press, Wasafiri, Modron Magazine, New Writing North and the Poetry Society.

MJ Hunter Brueggemann is Senior Lecturer in Fine Arts, Computational Arts and Creative Computing at the University of the Arts, London. They hold an interdisciplinary PhD in digital innovation (HighWireDTC) from Lancaster University. Hunter's primary research focuses on conflicts of knowledge systems, with academic foundations in science and technology studies, critical theory, methodology and non-representational and posthuman theories.

Yairen Jerez Columbié grew up in Havana. She works as Lecturer in Latin American and Caribbean Studies at University College Cork. Prior to this she was Assistant Professor in Latin American Studies and Intercultural Communication at Trinity College Dublin. She is the author of the monograph *Essays on Transculturation and Catalan-Cuban Intellectual History* (2021) and of the poetry collections *Fósiles de lluvia* (Betania, 2022) and *De corales* (Betania, 2024).

Koundinya Dhulipalla is an artist-developer and Lecturer in Art and Technology at UCL Slade School of Fine Art. Their practice explores software art, tool-building and the politics of technology in networked cultures.

Dilar Dirik is an organiser, writer and independent researcher. She holds a PhD in Sociology from the University of Cambridge. From 2019–23, she worked as a postdoctoral fellow at the University of Oxford. Her book, *The Kurdish Women's Movement: History, theory, practice* (Pluto Press 2022), is an in-depth ethnography of the revolutionary women's struggle in Kurdistan. Dilar has left academia and focuses on political education and internationalist alliance-building.

Dami Folayan is a Black woman Christian poet, theorist and sociologist. She holds a PhD from the University of Cambridge, looking at the experiences of Black women at Cambridge, past and present. She specialises in widening participation, Black-British womanhood and the sociology of education. She holds a BSc in Sociology and Education Studies and an MSc in International Social Change and Policy. Her interdisciplinary research explores 'how do we do Black womanhood in these spaces?'. Through narratives, critical poetic enquiry and creative arts-based research methods, her research seeks to centre the experiences of Black women at Oxbridge, working to understand how we cannot merely survive, but thrive. Dami's work positions higher education as a colonial city and explores how the colonial history of Oxbridge influences the lived experience of Black women.

Haydn Kirnon is Lecturer (Teaching) on the Spanish, Portuguese and Latin American Studies (SPLAS) programme at UCL, where he teaches translation. He has been a professional translator and subtitler for over 30 years and has worked as a lexicographer on several dictionaries for Oxford University Press, including the *Oxford Beginner's Spanish Dictionary*.

Dita N. Love is an interdisciplinary social scientist, educator and creative writer interested in abolitionist and generational approaches to education, social justice, collective liberation and institutional healing, led with, by and for often marginalised, minoritised and migrant communities. Her research focus spans youth education, creative methodologies and contemporary arts, centring live and digital poetry and performance. As Junior Research Fellow at Homerton, she is researching anti-oppressive creative community partnerships for widening access and participation in elite university spaces. Priorly, she has worked as ESRC Postdoctoral Research Fellow at the Faculty of Education, University of Cambridge, following a PhD in Education on spoken word, poetry and hip hop with imprisoned young men in the Balkans (Gates Cambridge Scholarship). Her writing has been published by the Oxford Review of Education, Australian Art Education, Mantis (Stanford University's journal of poetry, criticism and translation), Palgrave, and Routledge.

Shirley May is a first-generation Black British poet, from the Jamaican diaspora, and a proud Mancunian. As a member of the Royal Society of Literature and a fellow at Manchester Metropolitan University, she crafts evocative verses and leads as CEO and Artistic Director of Young

Identity. In this role, she mentors the city's youth, inspiring them to find their voices through poetry and performance. Her debut album, *Rainfall*, encapsulates the essence of poetry to music. Shirley's book, *She Wrote Her Own Eulogy*, is a profound blend of wisdom, memory, future and hope. Her poetry can be found in numerous anthologies.

Kerry McInerney (Ngāti Ruanui) is Lecturer in AI at the University of Auckland School of Computer Science and Associate Fellow at the Leverhulme Centre for the Future of Intelligence, University of Cambridge. Her work examines the intersections between race, gender, technology and politics. She is an AHRC/BBC Radio 3 New Generation Thinker, one of *Computing*'s 30 under 30, and one of the Top 100 Brilliant Women in AI Ethics 2022.

Mathelinda Nabugodi is Lecturer in Comparative Literature at UCL. Prior to this she was Leverhulme Trust Early Career Fellow in the Faculty of English at the University of Cambridge. In 2016, she was the first to be awarded a PhD in Creative Critical Writing from UCL. She has edited Shelley's translations from Aeschylus, Calderón and Goethe for *The Poems of Shelley: 1821–1822* as well as the essay collection *Thinking Through Relation: Encounters in creative critical writing*. Her critical memoir, *The Trembling Hand: Reflections of a Black woman in the Romantic archive* is due to be published by Hamish Hamilton (UK) and Knopf (US).

Marcin W. Smietana is Research Fellow at Ca' Foscari University of Venice (Italy) and Affiliated Lecturer at the University of Cambridge (UK). From 2014 to 2022, he was a postdoc Research Associate and Senior Research Associate in the Reproductive Sociology Research Group (ReproSoc) at the University of Cambridge. He has carried out research on LGBTQ+ families, queer kinships and the sociology of reproduction, surrogacy and pregnancy in the UK, the US, Spain and Poland.

Anna T. is an islander. She works as an artist, educator and curator in Vienna, Austria. She has taught at the Academy of Fine Arts Vienna, the University of Art and Design Linz, and the University of Vienna. Her artistic practice and scholarly work focus on language, migration and queerness. Since 2003 she has exhibited and participated in numerous group and solo exhibitions and new media festivals in Europe, the Americas and Australia, in her capacity as an artist, curator and organiser. She is the author of *Opacity – Minority – Improvisation: An exploration of the closet through queer slangs and postcolonial theory*. Her most recent book is *Δiotima; or, Δeir*land: A fragmented stori of arkivs, kolektivism, imagina/on, & multituds* (2025).

Bea Wohl's research focuses on digital innovation and inclusion. They have an MA in Media and Communications (European Graduate School), an Advanced Certificate in PR (Chartered Institute of Public Relations) and a MRes/PhD in Digital Innovation (Lancaster University). They were previously Post-Doctoral Fellow on Transforming the Gap: Inclusive Digital Arts and Humanities Research Skills CoLab.

Debbie Yeboah is a Ghanaian artist with a PhD from the Faculty of Education, University of Cambridge (Cambridge Trust Scholarship). Her research focuses on utilising contemporary African artwork as a pedagogical pathway towards decolonisation of curricula, allowing Africans and African diasporic people to rethink the dominant Western epistemological framing of both education and aesthetics, and feel empowered about who they are and where they come from. Her work conceptualises a new decolonial methodology and theory in art education, exploring themes of epistemic violence, repair and coloniality. Debbie is also an educational consultant, with a particular interest in curriculum development and reform, diversity and inclusion, and decolonial pedagogy. Previously Debbie worked in education in Ghana, for five years as an art and design teacher, at Primary and IGCSE levels, and in school management. She is also an artist, exploring painting and drawing techniques and styles, which are informed by her research practice. She recently stepped down as President of the Ghanaian Society of Cambridge University.

Acknowledgements

The Fire Now: Anti-racist scholarship in times of explicit racial violence (2018), co-edited by Beth Kamunge, Azeezat Johnson and Remi Joseph-Salisbury, has been a particularly strong influence on our work and Beth Kamunge generously contributed to one of our events, which was a great inspiration for us.

We are grateful to the volume contributors for entrusting their work to us and to the many people who thought through the guiding philosophy of this volume with us and participated in various seminar series and events detailed in the Introduction, especially the Creaction: Creative Critical Interventions for Social Justice series in Spring–Summer 2021, which was generously funded by The Leverhulme Trust, through Natasha Tanna's Early Career Fellowship (ECF-2019-558). Participants in the series included: Beth Kamunge, Sayak Valencia, Dorian Wood, Gabrielle Le Roux, Olumide Popoola, Syrus Marcus Ware, Lola Olufemi, Gülkan 'Noir', Gizem Oruç, Elmira and Ramona Zadissa. Beyond these workshops, Marcin Smietana was the co-organiser of numerous events that eventually developed into this project.

The life of this project has spanned various explicit acts of violence across the world, some of which are addressed in the chapters in this volume, which is obviously by no means exhaustive. The volume took shape organically through our workshops and collaborations, rather than us deciding in advance what topics would be included. Since the workshops in 2021, and since we first met with potential contributors to an edited volume, in January 2022, there have been major shifts in social justice practice and discourse (including a backlash with the resurgence of the far right in many parts of the world) and major injustices in this time. This volume's lack of direct engagement with some of these specific instances of violence and resistance does not reflect our view on the importance and urgency of these issues.

On a personal level, editors and contributors have been through moves in continent, job precarity, and numerous bereavements, and some of us have left academic institutions to engage in more activist work, much of which has shaped these chapters. As co-editors, we have endeavoured to keep care at the centre of the editorial process, conscious of the destructive force of a neoliberal drive for productivity regardless of social and personal context, as discussed by Tricia Hersey in *Rest is Resistance* (2022) and Maggie Berg and Barbara K. Seeber in *The Slow Professor: Challenging the culture of speed in the academy* (2016) and this has meant some inevitable delays in our process. We are grateful to the contributors and to UCL Press for their patience and understanding of this approach.

We also want to acknowledge the absences in this book; a couple of contributors who were due to write chapters for this volume were unable to complete them due to difficult personal circumstances, including increased precarity in academic employment. We feel those gaps in the volume.

As an editorial team we are grateful to the co-editor for the UCL Press Comparative Literature and Culture series, Timothy Mathews, for his encouragement prior to and during the long process of bringing this volume to life and to the reviewers of our book proposal, who made some excellent suggestions for additional interlocutors.

Introduction

Natasha Tanna, Abeyamí Ortega Domínguez and Hakan Sandal-Wilson

Creative Critical Interventions for Social Justice is an edited volume premised on an ethos of politically-engaged research that shifts beyond or questions traditional scholarly forms and norms. Feminist, queer and anti-racist scholars and activists have long challenged the claims to objectivity of the neutral voice of much scholarly writing and this volume builds on that work. The volume considers the sorts of knowledge that conventional academic production might exclude or marginalise and explores the potential for creative critical writing and cultural production to advance social-justice-focused research and practice. Contributions address hierarchies of knowledge production and knowledge producers, bringing together artists, curators, educators, community organisers, activists, researchers and writers, the majority of whom are also academics, who see their work as focusing on social justice from decolonial, anti-racist, queer and transfeminist perspectives.

The collection as a whole considers the role of storytelling and experimental, creative and often collaborative interventions across, between and beyond disciplines. Issues addressed in the volume include uses of poetry in youth and climate justice work, conversational life stories as a research method in sociological studies of kinship formation, reflections on the potentials and pitfalls of centring researcher positionality and lived experience as a basis for scholarly analysis, relationality and the ethics of ethnographic work with radical political movements, speculative imaginings of the future of political organising and notions of rigour and care for the living and the dead in racialised archives.

Bridging spheres: undisciplined disciplines, social poetics and *otherwise* academia

The bridging of artist, activist and academic spheres has been central to our work and indeed many contributors would consider themselves artists, activists and academics. However, we also want to acknowledge the challenges that may arise and that have arisen in our efforts to work across these different spheres, often due to economic/funding inequalities, imbalanced power dynamics and hierarchies that persist and emerge in the process of collaboration, as some of the chapters in this volume address (for example Chapter 7). Despite the discomfort and difficulties that attempts at ethical collaboration across these contexts might involve, we believe that such collaboration is vital for addressing social injustices. It is our view that scholarship benefits from deep engagement beyond the university, and we also believe that activist visions and perspectives benefit from collaboration with thinkers and scholar-activists within the university. Neither scholarly nor activist perspectives hold the absolute truth and we resist the idealisation and romanticisation of either sphere.

In terms of writing about, writing with and writing by different marginalised groups, our approach resonates with Mark Nowak's perspectives in *Social Poetics* (2020) on the 'committed author' versus political and poetic practices that engage working-class and other marginalised communities rather than purporting to represent them. In this volume, some chapters enact and discuss the sort of 'social poetics' that Nowak advocates, other chapters discuss the difficulties of scholar/activist relations across stubborn hierarchies. Some of the creative critical interventions discussed here bring to light imbalances in power and the volume seeks to put forward ways that power may be distributed more equitably. Drawing on Ngũgĩ wa Thiong'o in developing his argument, Nowak notes that:

> In an era when many communities of poetry continue to embed themselves deeper and deeper into elite institutions (private colleges and elite universities, costly academic conferences and writers retreats, black-tie book award ceremonies, and the like), social poetics remains a radically public poetics, a poetics for and by the working-class people who read it, analyze it, and produce it within their struggles to transform twenty-first century capitalism into a more equitable, equal and socialist system of relations. (Nowak 2020, 2)

Importantly, for Nowak, 'Social poetics seeks the transition of the pen or the laptop from the "committed author" (be they journalist, academic poet, novelist, playwright, or other writing professional) to working people themselves in a new conjunction of aesthetic practice and political action' (Nowak 2020, 7–8). Both in centring the work of queer and negatively racialised scholars and the work of scholar-activists with marginalised communities, we seek to centre the perspectives of those who have long been spoken *about* or *for* in scholarly writing. In some cases, this requires that researchers simply 'get out of the way' so that people and communities who have experienced violence, discrimination and marginalisation can more directly communicate their perspectives in their own words, a process which in itself may form part of an alternative route to justice, especially in the face of a lack of justice by more formal means. In other cases, more of a collaborative approach is beneficial, provided that researchers pay close attention to stubborn power dynamics. While we and the majority of our contributors often write in university contexts, we strive to be 'in but not of' the university, in Stefano Harney and Fred Moten's words (Harney and Moten 2013, 26). Of their book, Jack Halberstam notes the drive for connection beyond academia that characterises Harney and Moten's 'subversive intellectual': 'the subversive intellectual enjoys the ride and wants it to be faster and wilder; she does not want a room of his or her own, she wants to be in the world, in the world with others and making the world anew' (Halberstam 2013, 10).

The questioning of the centrality of the academic researcher and scholarly norms has led to various attempts to envision what some writers, activists and academics have termed knowledge production – or 'study' in Harney and Moten's terms (Harney and Moten 2013, 9) – 'otherwise'. Key works and projects that discuss and develop 'otherwise' approaches include Lola Olufemi's *Experiments in Imagining Otherwise* (2021) that bridges political organising and Black feminist scholarship; Danah Abdulla's 'Imagining otherwise' (2020); Laura McTighe and Megan Raschig's 'An otherwise anthropology' (2019); Cristina Rojas's 'International political economy/development otherwise' (2007) and *Otherwise*'s 'Otherwise manifesto' (2025). For Rojas, in the 'otherwise' scholarly space, 'different narratives [are brought] into contact with each other, allow[ing] the marginalized to reveal their own interpretation, and opens space for accommodation, contradiction, and resistance' (Rojas 2007, 585). The *Otherwise* manifesto includes a desire for shifting 'established positionalities of storytelling':

> We see Otherwise as an interface between storytellers of the ordinary within and outside academia, activism, professional writing, visual arts, and areas of life and work where opportunities for storytelling remain limited.
>
> We wish to question established positionalities of storytelling, and aim to create a space for the researched – and not only the researcher – to tell their stories. (Otherwise 2025)

We hope that this volume will contribute to social justice work *otherwise*, within and beyond the academy, with a constant process of reflection on how pernicious inequities may emerge in any case.

As well as spanning artist, activist and academic spheres, we have also sought to work across disciplinary divides that often persist within academia. The contributors to the volume come from different disciplinary backgrounds, including computing, modern languages, and gender studies, and as co-editors we also merge approaches from literary/cultural studies (Tanna), visual anthropology (Ortega Domínguez), and political sociology (Sandal-Wilson), with an acute awareness of the knowledges often overlooked within our respective disciplines. Following Halberstam in *A Queer Art of Failure* (2011), we agree that '[w]e may, ultimately, want more undisciplined knowledge, more questions and fewer answers' (Halberstam 2011, 10) and that 'we might go with the thicket of subjugated knowledge that sprouts like weeds among the disciplinary forms of knowledge, threatening always to overwhelm the cultivation and pruning of the intellect with mad plant life' (Halberstam 2011, 9).

By privileging creative ways of writing for social justice – or questioning the privilege of a specific academic norm, for that matter – the volume commits to feminist research principles. On the one hand, the contributions reflect on 'whether the analysis presented in the work reinscribes the researched into the dominant representations of powerlessness, into being viewed as without agency, into being defined as abnormal' (Bhavnani 1993, 98). As such, contributors engage in critical self-reflexivity as a form of personal and social accountability, aware of the limitations, challenges and contradictions inherent to the power relations and the hierarchical, privileged dynamics shaping the political economies of academic practices and their outcomes. We recognise our implication in elite institutions and potential complicities with power. In our approaches, creative critical engagement concerns not only ourselves as scholars and writers reflecting on the ethical implications of our own practices, it also involves thinking about the possibilities of co-creating in collaboration with communities with which we do social justice-oriented work. In this sense, the volume highlights issues of privilege and problematises lived experience as something that may have different implications for people working from a variety of research positions and those whose lived experiences have potentially been subjected to extractive exploitative practices.

However, we wish to move beyond acknowledgements of privilege that may lead to a form of paralysis or even an abdication of responsibility, plagued by thoughts such as 'who am I to speak / act?', or to statements that act as disclaimers, while research continues as it did before. In some cases, the most ethical act for researchers may be to step aside so other perspectives can take centre stage, as we mention above. However, many situations require more active collaboration, for example where scholar-activists might do behind-the-scenes groundwork to actively foster and create spaces for those whose stories are not heard, amplifying their perspectives. Returning again to Harney and Moten's *The Undercommons*, we are wary and weary of endless critique without action as well as action without critique. Indeed, they refer to the possible paralysis caused by endless critique and the subversive intellectual needing to 'retreat … into the external world'.

> The undercommons might by contrast be understood as wary of critique, weary of it, and at the same time dedicated to the collectivity of its future, the collectivity that may come to be its future. The undercommons in some ways tries to escape from critique and its degradation as university-consciousness and self-consciousness about university-consciousness, retreating, as Adrian Piper says, into the external world. (Harney and Moten 2013, 38)

We know that we will inevitably make mistakes in theory as praxis but seek not to be overcome by the paralysis of perfection or ethical/political/theoretical purism.

Rather than adhering to a binary logic that mobilises a conceptual geopolitical and sociocultural global divide, the volume engages, thinks, problematises and creates across positionalities and experiences of Global North and Global South, West and East, not merely as geographically confined phenomena, but as entangled multi-dimensional spheres. While we reject the generalising hierarchical notions of 'first' versus 'third' world, or 'developed' versus 'underdeveloped' countries, the chapters engage with interconnected differential economic realities and inequalities across the globe. In this way, the volume embraces a dynamic vision of bringing into dialogue actors from the various Souths – or social, economic, and cultural margins of the dominant political map – including those who are located, or transit, zones in various Norths.

The 'creaction' philosophy: What is 'creaction'? What work does 'social justice' as a concept do in this volume?

Through our conversations and the practices we have developed in this book, the concept of 'creaction' has been a grounding concept for the volume and was the title for a series of events at UCL's Institute of Advanced Studies in the spring and summer of 2021 that brought many of the contributors together. The ethos of Tanna, Ortega Domínguez and Sandal-Wilson's 'Creaction: Creative Critical Interventions for Social Justice' series included a focus on:

- politically engaged/social justice work that decentres or questions conventional scholarly forms;
- centring creativity, pleasure, and joy in knowledge production, even when working with difficult and painful issues, in order to counter the spectacle of violence that can result from an academic focus on lives located at various junctures of marginalisation and discrimination;
- addressing hierarchies of knowledge production and knowledge producers and bridging academia/activist/creative divide;
- questioning what 'rigour' means and how the term is deployed;
- thinking about experimental, creative, and collaborative ways of doing research, even when not technically doing what might be considered practice-based research.

In the spaces we have created that culminated in this volume, we have closely engaged with the concept of social justice, its promises and its limitations. Rather than defining what it is, we have examined the work 'social justice' does as a theoretical concept and a regulatory and disciplinary framework. We reflect on what 'social justice' can enable us to see and do when we engage it through creative interventions. For example, in the 'Queering Authoritarianisms: Conflict, Resistance, and Coloniality' conference, we explored how 'bringing together those who ask queer questions about issues pertaining to social justice' could help us 'interrogate power structures that enable racism, anti-Semitism, xenophobia, and poverty' (Sandal-Wilson and Smietana 2021). In the year-long research network, 'Global Conversations Towards Queer Social Justice', we adopted a 'broad approach to the notion of "social justice", which we underst[oo]d as including racial justice, climate justice, and human engagements with the more-than-human world' (Sandal-Wilson et al. 2021). It is this expansive vision that enabled us to weave different, and at times conflicting, visions of social justice that are context dependent. In the spirit of a commitment to social justice and acknowledging its limitations, and our own various positions towards it, with this volume we continue to seek ways to reflect on and emancipate the potential and the story of social justice 'differently rather than telling different stories' (Hemmings 2011, 16). We hope that 'social justice' can work, in this volume's case, as a call to different political visions and writing forms to come together to improve the conditions of humans and non-humans alike and help us demand justice collectively from our own differing locations vis-à-vis structures of domination, without a claim to a position of hegemonic authority or prescriptive definition of what counts as social justice.

Through creative forms, the contributions aim to expand a social-justice project that goes beyond the confines of academia, as well as the confines of narrowed imaginations of justice. As Linda Tuhiwai Smith reminds us: 'Research for social justice expands and improves the conditions for justice; it is an intellectual, cognitive, and moral project, often fraught, never complete, but worthwhile' (Smith 2022, 270). This volume, following similar ethics and commitment to justice, does not claim to bring about social justice through research and writing but aims to improve the conditions for it, through sustained critique and multiple forms that can touch people in various ways.

There has been ongoing dialogue among the contributors and co-editors about different scholarly forms that emerge from and foster social-justice-focused research, and a number of the chapters emerged from contributors' engagements with other events organised by the co-editors, from 2018 onwards, including:

1) 'Methods in Question: Epistemologies of Gender and Sexuality' convened by Hakan Sandal-Wilson, initially at the University of Cambridge (2018 onwards, https://methodsinquestion.co.uk/), including a collaborative piece by co-editors Hakan Sandal-Wilson and Natasha Tanna titled: 'The politics of writing in and with crises' (2020)

2) a creative critical workshop led by volume co-editor Natasha Tanna at the 'Queering Authoritarianisms: Conflict, Resistance, and Coloniality' conference at the University of Cambridge, which was organised by co-editor Hakan Sandal-Wilson and contributor Marcin Smietana (March 2021)
3) fortnightly creative events and workshops co-organised by co-editors Natasha Tanna and Hakan Sandal-Wilson along with contributor Marcin Smietana as part of the research network 'Global Conversations Towards Queer Social Justice' (September 2021–August 2022).

The ethos we developed for this series of events, in dialogue with participants and attendees, permeates this volume. For us, 'creaction', the bringing together of critical (denoted by the 'cr') + creative ('crea') + action, signifies 'creative critical actions focused on social justice', and we use it as a shorthand for such creative critical interventions. However, we appreciate that the term has other resonances and other significations (such as creation, reaction). Creaction can have a poetic dimension, especially if we consider the root of poiesis as a generative act of making. We find the gesture towards critical creation helpful given that a number of these social-justice-focused interventions seek to create more liveable worlds. Creaction denotes this creative act of emancipatory world-making through critical reflection and critical action, ever aware of the potential criticisms of such actions in turn.

The notion of a 'reaction' is complex and problematic, not least because it might conjure a sense of the 'reactionary', that is, a conservative response to progressive politics. Nonetheless, creaction can be a generative term as we engage the etymological root of reaction – acting again, a sign of persistence – in response to a stimulus or force. When the reaction is guided by a preoccupation or engagement with social justice/emancipatory practices from critical perspectives, we see it as a form of creaction. As such, our work might be considered to embrace reactions, in the sense of reacting to particular situations of injustice and fostering 'reactions' (thinking here of laboratories of chemical reactions) in the experimental interplay of artistic, activist and academic approaches.

However, the lingering possibility of 'reactionary' practice is perhaps also telling, given that creativity has not always been used for socially just or emancipatory ends.[1] The volume is critically aware of

[1] We thank the reviewers of the book proposal for their emphasis on this point.

the problematic entanglements between creative practices – including writing – with the production of neoliberal industrial logics and economies (see Brouillette 2014). We do not mean to suggest that creative practice is *inherently* liberatory, and note that it has a myriad of complex histories and trajectories in institutional and non-institutional settings across geographies. Indeed, some of the chapters reflect on the potential pitfalls and challenges of creative practice. For example, Chapter 5, 'Notes on lying', questions how an increase in negatively racialised scholars drawing creatively on their lived experience has, in some cases, led to the expectation or demand that such scholars make their personal histories legible in certain ways.

On form and rigorous mess

Through centring lived experience, engaging with experimental forms and spotlighting researcher positionality, this volume explores the limitations of conventional scholarly forms of writing. The chapters interrogate loaded notions of scholarly rigour, mastery and perfection. Contributors are concerned with what knowledges might be excluded where 'rigour' implies adherence to certain academic norms and forms, or as José Esteban Muñoz puts it, rigour as an 'institutional ideology' (Muñoz 1996, 7), rather than a focus on rigour of thought in a variety of formats. This volume demonstrates the rigour that might be present in alternative forms emerging from social-justice-related practice that have not necessarily been valued in academic contexts. These forms of rigour may be a way of 'bringing theory back to life', in Sara Ahmed's terms. For Ahmed, 'The personal is theoretical. Theory itself is often assumed to be abstract: something is more theoretical the more abstract it is, the more it is abstracted from everyday life. To abstract is to drag away, detach, pull away, or divert. We might then have to drag theory back, to bring theory back to life' (Ahmed 2017, 10). Ahmed talks about how, through engaging with the work of Audre Lorde, bell hooks, Gloria Anzaldúa and other feminists of colour, she 'began to appreciate that theory can do more the closer it gets to the skin' (Ahmed 2017, 10). Similarly, for Olufemi: 'Theory can be lived, held, shared. It is a breathing, changeable thing that can be infused in many political and artistic forms' (Olufemi 2020, 7). The chapters in this volume seek to bring theory to life.

The ethos guiding this volume envisions social-justice-oriented academic work as a politically-charged critical, creative intervention. This approach emphasises what we see as porous engagements: an expanded, interconnected, multi-directional, mutually influential practice that navigates different realities and positionalities in complex, permeable and, importantly, problematic ways (Rivera Cusicanqui 2012). In this sense, we embrace Donna Haraway's invitation to 'stay with the trouble' (2016). The contributions to the volume reflect on how academic form is political and explore how writing and research methodologies might reflect uncertainty, doubt, passion and collaboration – with the learnings that come while erring at these attempts – through an engagement with more experimental critical forms. While encouraging these experimental approaches, we remain aware of the potential pitfalls of the postmodern questioning of the notion of 'truth' and the pressure to produce more with less time that has resulted in a reduction in time for many researchers to engage in long-form thought, which remains important to defend. In our focus on creativity, pleasure and care we have also been inspired by the forms of creative solidarity fostered through the Tactics and Praxis workshops convened by Isabelle McNeill, Georgina Evans and Louise Haywood, which created spaces for 'creativity, play, slowness, and pleasure' (2018) and their accompanying manifesto (2020).

Our work has drawn inspiration from *The Fire Now: Anti-racist scholarship in times of explicit racial violence* (Johnson et al. 2018). We have been particularly inspired by Beth Kamunge's observations that 'being in the middle of a fire can make any type of writing generally, and succinct, coherent thought in particular, a privilege only available to some' (Kamunge et al. 2018, 189–90). In her questioning about 'Who gets to write while the fire is happening?' (Kamunge et al. 2018, 193), Kamunge notes that 'publishing standards tend to construct detached, "objective", "rational", inaccessible writing as good writing', asking: 'Is there room for "messy" writing that calls for speculation? That poses more questions than it does answers? That embodies grief and lament …?' (Kamunge 2018, 190). Some of the chapters in this volume seek to respond to this question through exploring writing with a sense of emotional immediacy, doubt and imagination that may not always be 'polished' or 'coherent' in form.

We join Alyosxa Tudor's analysis that the global targeting of 'emancipatory fields of knowledge production' (Tudor 2020, 239) such as the decolonising movement, feminist queer scholarship and gender studies, as a sustained critique, are intertwined. Resistance to global and connected attacks on these fields requires an equally intertwined, messy approach (Tudor 2020, 239). Other works and concepts that have inspired our attention to messy interconnectedness are Gloria Anzaldúa's 'el mundo zurdo' (left-handed world) (Anzaldúa 2002, 232), part of her borderland theory in which those who inhabit the borderlands, or in-between spaces, characterised by an alienation from normative spheres, co-exist and co-create new worlds; Remi Joseph-Salisbury and Laura Connelly's *Anti-Racist Scholar-Activism* (2021); Harney and Moten's *The Undercommons* (2013) and Sandeep Bakshi, Suhraiya Jivraj and Silvia Posocco's *Decolonizing Sexualities* (2016).

Cristina Rivera Garza discusses the labour involved in preserving mess and vitality in writing:

> Hay que trabajar mucho para producir una escritura en sucio. Hay que evitar el proceso convencional que lleva a la página cocida: matar a la presa (lo real) y cocinarlo (sacarle el jugo) de tal modo que se convierta en una entidad perfecta, sí, pero inerte y sin vida. Hay que resistir la versión final y conservar, siempre, la posibilidad de que eso que saltó una vez hacia la percepción lo vuelva a hacer desde la página. (Rivera Garza 2009)

> It takes a lot of work to produce messy writing. You have to avoid the conventional process that leads to the cooked page … that kills its prey (the real) and cooks it (draining it of its juices) in such a way that it converts it into a perfect entity, perfect, yes, but inert and lifeless. We have to resist the final version and preserve always the possibility that what jumped into our minds, our perception, can do that for readers from the page. (Our translation)

Echoing this valorisation of 'mess', the volume does not argue for a uniform, homogenous approach to scholarly forms. Rather it seeks to explore the different ways in which critical modes of writing might be stretched and challenged in social-justice projects and research that seek to engage with knowledges that might not fit into standard academic forms. It seeks to demonstrate how rigour of thought might manifest in a variety of ways, and that conflating 'rigour' with adherence to particular modes of writing might itself be considered as an approach lacking rigour. As such, the coherence of the volume manifests in shared aims relating to social justice, rather than a homogenous approach or way of writing. Some of the chapters are more serious in tone, whereas others are lighter (for example Chapter 3) despite, or perhaps because of, the seriousness of their content – humour, or being 'frivolous', can be a powerful form of rigour, as Halberstam notes in *The Queer Art of Failure*: 'terms like *serious* and *rigorous* tend to be code words, in academia as well as other contexts, for disciplinary correctness; they signal a form of training and learning that confirms what is already known according to approved methods of knowing, but they do not allow for visionary insights or flights of fancy' (2011, 6). Halberstam instead advocates for 'los[ing] one's way' (6), which resonates with the 'messiness' that we have valorised as part of the creaction philosophy.

Through its critical engagement with scholarly rigour, traditional scholarly forms and writing conventions, the volume aims to contribute to the decolonial and postcolonial critique of 'research through imperial eyes' (Smith 2022, 49–65). This critique focuses on how a specific Western epistemological position determines all aspects of research through its own presumptions about life, politics and ideas (Smith 2022, 63), and how it can impact the political economies of writing practices (Nadal 2021; Nadiminti 2018). Accordingly, this volume calls for sustained attention to the creation and communication of research and practice for social justice that challenges or pushes at the limits of conventional scholarly forms of writing. Below we outline the chapters within the four parts of the volume, with attention to poetry, conversation and life storytelling, positionality and relationality in research, and the racial and colonial politics of digital and physical archives, with a return to poetry again in the final chapter, to take us full circle.

Summary of parts and chapters

The chapters in Part I, 'Poetic possibilities for youth and climate justice' forward the volume's aim of considering the power of poetry and creative, collaborative interventions in contexts of social injustice. This part of the volume focuses specifically on written and spoken-word poetry as creative critical forms and the processes behind its creation in two different contexts: as a response to the climate crisis and as a form of educational justice through taking seriously marginalised young people's radical imagination.

In Chapter 1, 'Paradoxically, writing ecopoetry: a reflection on creative tools, knowledge and change', Yairen Jerez Columbié discusses poetry as a form of scholarship, bringing together lived experience and social realities. In the face of the 'psychological climate paradox' – fatigue and apathy in response to media communication relating to the climate crisis while its effects become increasingly evident – the chapter argues that poetry might better increase the public's concern for climate justice.

In Chapter 2, '"Britishness is not Whiteness": youth poets "bite back" at the education survival complex through a killjoy call-and-response towards creative abolition', Dita N. Love, Debbie Yeboah, Dami Folayan and Shirley May explore the effect of youth engagement with Manchester-based youth poet Princess Arinola Adegbite aka P. A. Bitez, an alumna of arts charity Young Identity. The charity partnered with the Poetic Justice Values project to examine issues of educational justice and how spoken-word poetry can be harnessed in formal or non-formal education as a feminist killjoy praxis based on Black radical creativity that is anti-colonial, anti-carceral and anti-capitalist.

Moving on from poetry as creative critical method, Part II, 'Conversations for change: life stories of Black, queer and trans kinship and parenthood' centres the life stories and lived experiences of Black, queer, and trans parenthood and kinship. The emphasis on storytelling opens up space for marginalised voices, not as marginalised voices but as actors capable of telling their own stories.

In Chapter 3, 'Heather and Maggie', Haydn Kirnon enacts the creaction approach through life storytelling. He celebrates the formative impact of queer friendship as a form of kinship that is often particularly heightened during adolescence, demonstrating how storytelling might help us honour the lives and impact of queer kin. The chapter's conversational tone – Halberstam discusses 'analysis as a mode of conversation, *rather than mastery*' (Halberstam 2011, 12) – and use of humour enact a form of knowledge production and memory creation that recognises and celebrates aspects of queer life that may be obscured or omitted in more conventional academic essays.

In Chapter 4, '"If you're gay, you're lucky to be a parent": current issues for queer and trans families in the UK', Marcin Smietana engages with the creaction philosophy by centring lived experience in bringing to the fore the routes to parenthood and parenting experiences of five queer and trans parent-activists. As in Chapter 3, this chapter also centres the voices and experiences of actors themselves to question 'parenthood' as a normative institution and show multiple and often messy forms of parenthood and reproductive pathways. Thus, resonating with the volume's aims of exploring unconventional forms, the form Smietana is engaging with here is both the stylistic form of the chapter and the form of parenthood itself. Through highlighting parents becoming activists because of their parenthood experience, Smietana and the parent-activists highlight the emergence of politics in an unexpected site.

Building on Part II's concerns with conversation and life storytelling as research methods, Part III of the volume, 'Paradox and parody:

the politics of positionality and relationality', explores when social-justice-focused research and artistic practice might fall prey to the same power dynamics that it seeks to resist. The three chapters playfully and politically address the possibilities and potential pitfalls of discussing and/or centring researcher positionality and relationality in social-justice-focused research. Despite its best intentions, such research must acknowledge not only its limitations, but also its potential violence and inevitable entanglements with historic and contemporary inequalities and fraught relations of privilege and precarity.

In Chapter 5, 'Notes on lying', Mathelinda Nabugodi considers the unintended effects of negatively racialised people generating knowledge from 'lived experience' in a move that challenges the alleged objectivity of rigorous scholarly thought. In this way, the chapter addresses the volume's questions around what 'rigour' means. When 'lived experience' rather than disembodied thought becomes an expectation, or even a demand, made of certain researchers, when they are expected to reveal much of themselves in this grounding of knowledge in experience, might dissimulation be valid? This chapter explores what might unfold when we set the demands for scholarly rigour against an anti-colonial push back to the Global North's intrusive and mastering gaze in relation to racialised knowledge producers.

In Chapter 6, 'Queer Mediterranean futures: an {uneventful} performative text', Anna T. reflects upon two key questions that are central to the volume's interest: positionality and relationality. This chapter problematises these two aspects by mobilising a self-reflexive approach that brings into dialogue different histories and temporalities of migration dynamics and political social movements in the Mediterranean. Through the embedding of differently positioned narratorial voices – using a blend of language styles, slang terms and future neologisms – this contribution evokes diverse voices and attempts to imagine a Southeastern European tale from the future.

In Chapter 7, 'The interview: scholarship, sincerity, suspicion', Dilar Dirik speaks to the themes of illegibility as epistemic resistance from Chapter 5 to think about the desire to be unresearchable as a form of survival in the context of the Kurdish women's liberation movement. Engaging with the volume's interest in what 'rigour' looks like, the chapter asks the following questions: How do certain forms of 'rigour' risk exposing or undermining the work of radical or revolutionary political movements and those taking part in them? What happens when researchers erase political and ideological analyses of their interlocutors while advancing their own careers? Who benefits from this research and, despite many researchers' best intentions, who might inadvertently be exposed to violence and surveillance? This chapter explores the ethical and political dilemmas around research into anti-systemic political movements. The dynamics, satirised through differently positioned narrative voices, highlight frequent boundary-crossing by researchers as well as the ideological, secular liberalism within academia that precludes the understanding and advancement of revolutionary perspectives.

Part IV, 'Reparative rigour: caring for the archives of the living and the dead', complicates the boundary between the living and the non-living (or the dead) by engaging with the interaction between the two. Aligning with the creaction philosophy, the form of these contributions challenges notions of rigour requiring objectivity or detachment by highlighting the researcher as an affective part of the 'big picture', as a gesture toward healing historical and contemporary violence through the creative forms of social-justice-focused research.

In Chapter 8, 'Writing at the limits of reason' MJ Hunter Brueggemann, Bea Wohl and Koundinya Dhulipalla put nonlinearity, more-than-rationality and restorative epistemic justice in tension through form as an activator of critical content, in dialogue with the volume's critique of the limitations of conventional scholarly styles of writing, the politics of form, and how writing methodologies might reflect uncertainty as queer practice. The chapter proposes to generate a philosophical reflection through art and writing, questioning the limits between prose and poetry, words and code, in order to destabilise the text and the textures of language. It thus deploys an exercise in emancipating obsolete forms of rigour and form in order to affirm its own emergent practices of rigorous queer writing.

In line with this book's concern with the forms of social-justice research as anti-racist practice, Chapter 9, 'the smell of rain on hot concrete', explores the potential and the failures of archives, literature, research and acts of remembrance to enact justice and care. Kerry McInerney charts how the racist murder of the New Zealand Chinese man, Joe Kum Yung, has been memorialised in archives, in literary responses to his death, in public fascination and remembrance and in McInerney's own bodily archive during her research. In this way McInerney engages with the volume's aims of considering the interplay of form and social justice to reflect on creative forms that might work with and against the archival grain to challenge racist violence, as well as centring the impact of researcher positionality.

Through these varied contributions we hope to give a snapshot into possibilities for creative critical interventions that have social justice at their heart, especially since creativity itself, particularly in institutionalised settings, is not inherently emancipatory. Some of the pieces enact creative practice, while others describe and analyse creative interventions, thinking about their possibilities and pitfalls – some do both. We hope that they will inspire future work for social justice in/and knowledge creation that questions, rejects, probes and/or plays with conventional academic form.

References

Abdulla, Danah. 2020. 'Imagining otherwise'. In *Decolonizing: The curriculum, the museum, and the mind*, 84–97. Vilnius: Vilnius Academy of Arts Press, 2020.

Ahmed, Sara. 2017. *Living a Feminist Life*. Durham, NC: Duke University Press.

Anzaldúa, Gloria. 2002 [1981]. 'La prieta'. In *This Bridge Called My Back: Writings by radical women of color*, edited by Cherríe Moraga and Gloria Anzaldúa, 220–33. Berkeley, CA: Third Woman Press.

Bakshi, Sandeep, Suhraiya Jivraj and Silvia Posocco (eds). 2016. *Decolonizing Sexualities: Transnational perspectives, critical interventions*. Oxford: Counterpress.

Berg, Maggie and Barbara Karolina Seeber. 2016. *The Slow Professor: Challenging the culture of speed in the academy*. Toronto: University of Toronto Press.

Bhavnani, Kum-Kum. 1993. 'Tracing the contours: Feminist research and feminist objectivity', *Women's Studies International Forum* 16(2): 95–104.

Brouillette, Sarah. 2014. *Literature and the Creative Economy*. Stanford, CA: Stanford University Press.

Halberstam, Jack. 2011. *The Queer Art of Failure*. Durham, NC: Duke University Press.

Halberstam, Jack. 2013. 'The wild beyond: with and for the undercommons'. In *The Undercommons: Fugitive planning and black study*, by Stefano Harney and Fred Moten, 2–13. New York: Minor Compositions.

Haraway, Donna J. 2016. *Staying with the Trouble: Making kin in the Chthulucene*. Durham, NC: Duke University Press.

Harney, Stefano and Fred Moten. 2013. *The Undercommons: Fugitive planning and black study*. Brooklyn: Minor Compositions.

Hemmings, Clare. 2011. *Why Stories Matter: The political grammar of feminist theory*. Durham, NC: Duke University Press.

Hersey, Tricia. 2022. *Rest is Resistance: Free yourself from grind culture and reclaim your life*. London: Aster.

Johnson, Azeezat, Remi Joseph-Salisbury and Beth Kamunge (eds). 2018. *The Fire Now: Anti-racist scholarship in times of explicit racial violence*. London: Zed Books.

Joseph-Salisbury, Remi and Laura Connelly. 2021. *Anti-Racist Scholar-Activism*. Manchester: Manchester University Press.

Kamunge, Beth, Wambui Mwangi and Osop Abdi Ali. 2018. 'Writing in the fire now: Beth dialogues with Wambui and Osop'. In *The Fire Now: Anti-racist scholarship in times of explicit racial violence*, edited by Azeezat Johnson, Remi Joseph-Salisbury and Beth Kamunge, 189–97. London: Zed Books.

McNeill, Isabelle, Louise Haywood and Georgina Evans. 2018. 'Tactics and praxis seminar series'. Accessed 28 March 2025. https://www.tacticsandpraxis.org/.

McNeill, Isabelle, Louise Haywood and Georgina Evans. 2020. 'Tactics and praxis: A manifesto'. In *MAI: Feminism and Visual Culture* 5. Accessed 7 October 2025. https://www.maifeminism.com/tactics-and-praxis-a-manifesto/.

McTighe, Laura and Megan Raschig. 2019. 'An otherwise anthropology', Society for Cultural Anthropology. Accessed 28 March 2025. https://culanth.org/fieldsights/series/an-otherwise-anthropology.

Muñoz, José Esteban. 1996. 'Ephemera as evidence: Introductory notes to queer acts', *Women & Performance: A journal of feminist theory* 8(2): 5–16.
Nadal, Paul. 2021. 'Cold War remittance economy: US creative writing and the importation of New Criticism into the Philippines', *American Quarterly* 73(3): 557–95.
Nadiminti, Kalyan. 2018. 'The Global Program era: Contemporary international fiction in the American creative economy', *Novel* 51(3): 375–98.
Nowak, Mark. 2020. *Social Poetics*. Minneapolis, MN: Coffee House Press.
Olufemi, Lola. 2020. *Feminism, Interrupted: Disrupting power*. London: Pluto Press.
Olufemi, Lola. 2021. *Experiments in Imagining Otherwise*. London: Hajar Press.
Otherwise. 2025. 'Otherwise Manifesto'. Accessed 28 March 2025. https://www.otherwisemag.com/magazine.
Rivera Cusicanqui, Silvia. 2012. 'Ch'ixinakax utxiwa: a reflection on the practices and discourses of decolonization', *South Atlantic Quarterly* 111(1): 95–109.
Rivera Garza, Cristina. 2009. 'La página cruda' [blog post]. *No Hay Tal Lugar*, 19 May. Accessed 28 March 2025. https://cristinariveragarza.blogspot.com/2009/05/.
Rojas, Cristina. 2007. 'International political economy/development otherwise', *Globalizations* 4(4): 573–87. https://doi.org/10.1080/14747730701695836.
Sandal-Wilson, Hakan and Marcin Smietana. 2021. '"Queering authoritarianisms": A queer rethinking of social justice and global politics' [blog post]. CRASSH. Accessed 28 March 2025. https://www.crassh.cam.ac.uk/blog/queering-authoritarianisms-a-queer-rethinking-of-social-justice-and-global/.
Sandal-Wilson, Hakan, Marcin Smietana and Natasha Tanna. 2021. 'Global conversations towards queer social justice' [blog post]. CRASSH. Accessed 28 March 2025. https://www.crassh.cam.ac.uk/research/networks/global-conversations-towards-queer-social-justice-2021-22/.
Sandal-Wilson, Hakan and Natasha Tanna. 2020. 'The politics of writing in and with crises: A conversation with Dr Natasha Tanna' [blog post]. *Methods in Question*. Accessed 28 March 2025. https://methodsinquestion.co.uk/blog/f/the-politics-of-writing-in-and-with-crisis.
Smith, Linda Tuhiwai. 2022 [1999]. *Decolonizing Methodologies: Research and indigenous peoples*. London: Bloomsbury Academic.
Tanna, Natasha, Abeyamí Ortega Domínguez and Hakan Sandal-Wilson. 2021. 'Creaction: Creative critical interventions for social justice' [workshop description]. Institute of Advanced Studies. Accessed 28 March 2025. https://www.ucl.ac.uk/institute-of-advanced-studies/news/2021/apr/creaction-creative-critical-interventions-social-justice.
Tudor, Alyosxa. 2020. 'Decolonizing trans/gender studies: Teaching gender, race and sexuality in times of the rise of the global right', *Transgender Studies Quarterly* 8(2).

Part I

Poetic possibilities for youth and climate justice

1
Paradoxically, writing ecopoetry: a reflection on creative tools, knowledge and change

Yairen Jerez Columbié

Introduction: outlining paradoxes

The walls of the city of Girona, close to the Iberian Peninsula's northern Mediterranean coast, are covered in fossilised unicellular creatures that inhabited ancient tropical seas millions of years ago. Visible to the bare human eye and often the size of a coin, the remains of these big cells are a reminder of our common origin in the ocean. The *pedra de Girona* (Girona stone), abundant in the old part of the city and on its medieval walls, is a type of limestone formed mainly by *nummulites*, which take their name from the Latin word '*nummulus*' (coin). They flourished in warm shallow tropical waters of the Tethys Sea, which ran from the centre of Europe to the Himalayas, more than 60 million years ago (see Fortey 2009). In summer 2014, I visited a private collection of fossils in my temporary neighbourhood in Girona. They were all beautiful and changed my relationship not only with the city but also with stones – now I am more inclined to notice '*los círculos que prueban / que una piedra es la huella de algo más*' – the circles that prove / a stone is the footprint of something else (Jerez Columbié 2022, 16).[1] As a tropical creature myself, born, raised and educated in Havana, Cuba, I then found a more embodied connection with a foreign city that had once been part of an equatorial sea. Until then, Girona had appealed to me mainly, and perhaps solely, through its language and history. This encounter with

[1] All the English translations of my poems provided in this chapter are by Matthew Geden. A poet, translator and creative writing teacher, Matthew Geden was born and brought up in the English Midlands, moving to Kinsale, Ireland in 1990. His poetry collections include *The Place Inside* (2012), *Fruit* (2020) and, most recently, *The Cloud Architect* (2022).

fossils led to some draft poems in Catalan and in Cuban Spanish; but the main work resulting from the experience would be a book of poetry whose title was inspired by what I thought was the most impressive piece in the collection of stones: a segment of fossilised rain.

Fósiles de lluvia – Fossilised rain – was published by Betania, in Madrid in May 2022, through a Trinity Association and Trust Grant. It is a book of ecopoetry written between Cuba, Catalonia and Ireland, which brings forward the relations between the cultures and natures of the Atlantic World in a context of climate change and related socio-ecological challenges. Migration, displacement, life cycles, destruction, resistance and transformation, are the main topics linking the texts, in which the poetic subjects interrogate both the material and the spiritual or more-than-human worlds of the Americas and Europe. In this chapter, I explore my creative process and provide flash translations as versions, imprints or fossils of the original poems written in Cuban Spanish. I combine essay writing and *autohistoria* – self-history – firstly to revisit the act of writing poetry, and secondly, to approach the poems, as both objects of study and research tools that use observation and creative practice, not only to explore but also to bring into being images, sounds and embodied experiences through *poiesis*, understood here as the human ability to create. Most specifically, I apply Gloria Anzaldúa's (2015) methodology of *autohistoria-teoría* (self-history-theory), the act of theorising on the practice of connecting lived experience with social realities, through a reflection on both my own involvement in creative practice and the role of poetry in academia and in wider society.

An article, published in the journal *Nature*, by researchers William Cassata and Paul Renne in 2012, analysed fossil imprints suggesting that it rained 2.7 billion years ago. This information highlights a long-standing palaeoclimate paradox. Around 2.7 billion years ago, the young sun's energy output was less than 85 per cent of that today. Such a faint sun would not have been able to warm Earth's surface above the freezing point of water and make rain possible, yet fossilised rain indicates that liquid water abounded at that time. More than ten years after the publication of Cassatas's and Renne's research, we continue to face a different yet related paradox. As underscored by Espen Stoknes in the book *What We Think about When We Try Not to Think about Global Warming* (2015), increasing scientific research, explaining how humans have caused changes to climate, has led to a decreasing concern in sections of the public, particularly in the so-called Global North, contributing to the 'psychological climate paradox'. Although climate science has provided ever more reliable data and models over the last 20 to 30 years, public concern for climate change is still insufficient to support ambitious policies. Conventional climate communication strategies have failed to resolve this contradiction. The final paradox framing my analysis is related to the fact that although novels, short stories, plays, lyrical essays and poems are central to the curricula and to the existence of modern languages and cultural studies departments in higher education, writing creatively is still considered a lesser form of academic contribution, and it is often disregarded by selection and promotion committees as a form of scholarship, in some contexts.

Moved by these paradoxes, I have recurred to poetry as both an applied practice and a form of scholarship that has linguistic experimentation as its main research tool, and *poiesis* – the human capacity to create and transform – at the centre of its research methodology. According to Stephen K. Levine (2020), *poiesis* is traditionally thought of as referring solely to artmaking, but it has the wider significance of shaping the world in response to human needs. In agreement with his latter view, I combine linguistic experimentation and *poiesis* to both evoke and create images, sounds, embodied experiences and *conocimiento* (insight and knowledge), which allow me to deepen understandings of a rapidly changing world while, probably in a subtle but also constant manner, reshaping it through my interactions with others – readers, colleagues, students and kin within the environment (see Anzaldúa 2015). In the following pages, I draw upon my limited yet sustained experience as a poet throughout the past decade in different socioecological systems – my urban coastal community in Havana, Cuba; the Costa Brava, in Catalonia; and the Lee's riverbank in Cork, Ireland – to exemplify how poetry is a form of scholarship. This exemplification aims to contribute to ongoing conversations by poet-scholars, academics and practitioners who are making a case for the role of poetry, in particular, and creative writing in general, within Modern Languages and Cultural Studies academic units, as well as within wider interdisciplinary environmental studies endeavours.[2]

[2] Some of these conversations took place in my own institution, University College Cork, among poet-scholars who participated in the one-day symposium Ecopoetry as Activism, Climate Action and Interdisciplinary Environmental Knowledge-Making, celebrated on 9 April 2024, with the participation of Indigenous Zoque poet Mikeas Sánchez as the keynote speaker. Mikeas Sánchez plays an integral role in the organisation Indigenous Zoque Faith-Based Movement in Defense of Life and Earth (ZODEVITE, for its Spanish initials), which challenges multiple extractive industries threatening traditional Zoque lands in southern Mexico: mining, oil fracking, hydroelectric dams, natural-gas drilling and geothermal power. ZODEVITE was awarded the 2017 Pax Christi International Prize for its non-violent resistance to mining and fracking. Her collected poems are available in the trilingual collection in Zoque, Spanish and English, titled *How to Be a Good Savage and Other Poems* (2024).

Reading and writing ecopoetry as scholarship and applied practice

My simultaneously theoretical and applied focus on ecopoetry is an invitation to think and feel beyond the Anthropocene, by interrogating diverse human experiences within nature through both observation and fabulation. This approach is informed by ongoing debates on humans' diverse positionings within the environment, which scrutinise the term Anthropocene, coined by Paul Crutzen and Eugene Stoermer (2000) to describe the current socioecological era as a geological epoch characterised by humans' acceleration of environmental degradation. Feeling the need for alternatives to the depoliticised concept of Anthropocene, which fails to acknowledge the different roles that diverse human communities play in relation to climate change, I bear in mind terms such as Capitalocene, Misanthropocene, Phallocene or Plantationocene, which invite us to consider the intersecting forms of classist, gender-based and colonial violence framing differential vulnerability and responsibilities in relation to climate change. Whereas Jason Moore (2016) has proposed 'Capitalocene' to highlight the ties between climate change and capitalism, Raj Patel (2013) has used 'Misanthropocene' to call attention to the misanthropy and racism that characterises some disaster responses and David Cole (2021) has built upon radical feminist perspectives to coin the term 'Phallocene' and suggest that we are living in a post-trust context shaped by patriarchy and misinformation. My work also often echoes the term 'Plantationocene', proposed by Donna Haraway (2015) and Malcom Ferdinand (2019) to acknowledge the role of the plantation system, colonisation and slavery in the acceleration of global warming. In this light, I consider that both the practice and the study of ecopoetry can also help us to interrogate the technocratic language that permeates environmental policies and discourses. My understanding of the term is aligned with J. Scott Bryson's definition:

> ecopoetry is a mode that, while adhering to certain conventions of traditional nature poetry, advances beyond that tradition and takes on distinctly contemporary problems and issues, thus becoming generally marked by three primary characteristics: an ecological and biocentric perspective recognizing the independent nature of the world; a deep humility with regard to our relationships with human and nonhuman nature; and an intense skepticism toward hyperrationality, a skepticism that usually

> leads to condemnation of an overtechnologized modern world and a warning concerning the very real potential of ecological catastrophe. (Bryson 2005, 2)

Despite most of them never using the epithet to refer either to themselves or others, it is easy to recognise the characteristics outlined by Bryson in some of the contemporary ecopoets that continue to influence my own work, such as Kamau Brathwaite (1973; 2005), Mary Oliver (1995) or Mikeas Sánchez (2024). From these poets, I have learnt, for instance, the importance of attention, movement and action for writing and discovery: 'And I walk on, over the shoulder of summer and down across the red-dappled fall; and, when it's late winter again, out through the far woodlands of the Provincelands, maybe another few hundred miles, looking for the owl's nest, yes, of course, and looking at everything else along the way' (Oliver 1995, 22). The acts of looking for, looking at, and looking within nature are central to my own understanding of ecopoetry. Walking is not a choice but a necessity for someone with motion sickness, an aversion towards driving, and living in a province with limited public transport options. However, my writing is not only widely informed by my poetic subjects' hikes – '*A diario alguien camina sobre flores detenidas / y piensa que son granos de arena*' – Every day someone walks on frozen flowers / and thinks they are grains of sand (Jerez Columbié 2022, 16) – but also by other motion experiences, both real and imagined:

> *Una figura se hunde en el paisaje.*
> *El agua hasta las rodillas*
> *abanica la luz sobre el cuerpo desnudo*
> *que la oleada impulsa*
> *a una marcha indecisa.*
> (Jerez Columbié 2022, 12)
>
> A figure sinks into the seascape.
> Knee-deep water reflects light
> all over the naked body
> ripples surge forward
> on an unknown path.

Similarly, and beyond stereotypes that could overestimate the centrality of music in some Caribbean people's lives, I see dancing as an important language itself, which a teacher taught me as a child, in

1990s Havana, to express feelings for which I still lacked the words. Therefore, the rhythm that both accompanies and provokes movements of the body, the mind and the imagination, is often apparent in my use of sound and the white page, as evinced in the poem with which I close this chapter. A familiar rhythm and movement also brightly animate the Caliban imagined by Kamau Brathwaite. The poetic subject, perhaps like the poet himself, walks and recreates my city of Havana and other recognisable Caribbean environments. Unlike Shakespeare's (2009) inarticulate character, Brathwaite's Caliban has a voice comparable to an orchestra, which combines percussion, string, brass and woodwind instruments with vocal cords, to vividly communicate in song the act of both walking and dancing through Caribbean histories and spaces:

> In Havana that morning, as every morning,
> the police toured the gambling houses
> wearing their dark glasses
> and collected tribute;
>
> (…) It was December second, nineteen fifty-six.
> It was the first of August eighteen thirty-eight.
> It was the twelfth October fourteen ninety-two.
>
> How many bangs how many revolutions?
>
> And
> Ban
> Ban
> Cal-
> iban
> like to play
> pan
> at the Car-
> nival;
> pran-
> cing up to the lim-
> bo silence
> down
> down
> so the god won't drown
> him

down
down
down
to the is-
land town
(Brathwaite 1973, 191–2)

The poem titled 'Caliban' is the third one in the section 'Limbo' of Brathwaite's collection *Islands*, first published in 1969 and later included in his trilogy *The Arrivants: A New World trilogy* (1973). The text refers to 1950s Havana and the landing of the Granma yacht, on 2 December 1956, which reinitiated the armed revolution led by Fidel Castro. The second date, 1 August 1838, refers to Emancipation Day, which marks the final date in the gradual abolition of slavery in the British Empire; and the last one, 12 October 1492, refers to Christopher Columbus's arrival on Caribbean shores and the so-called New World. These three historical moments would differently reshape the socio-historical landscapes of the Americas in the fifteenth, nineteenth and twentieth centuries. Impacted by these events himself, Brathwaite's Caliban takes over the sounds of violence in the second part of the poem; the ban[g]s of violence become both part of his name and the sound of the claves[3] marking the vital rhythm he embodies. Instantly, the limbo in the title of this book section transcends its biblical connotations to fully reveal itself as the resistance and survival dance of enslaved Africans and Afro-descendants in the Caribbean:

And limbo stick is the silence in front of me
limbo

limbo
limbo like me
limbo
limbo like me

[3] The *claves* are musical percussion instruments widely used in Cuba and in other Latin American and Caribbean countries. They consist of a pair of cylindrical hardwood sticks about eight inches (20 centimetres) long which, when struck together, produce a dry, bright, high-pitched sound with short sustain. The Spanish word *clave* also means 'key' or 'code'.

long dark night is the silence in front me
limbo
limbo like me
(Brathwaite 1973, 194)

In a recording of a Segue Reading at the Bowery Poetry Club in New York City,[4] on 1 May 2004, we can hear Kamau Brathwaite singing the lines above, before interrupting his melodic rendering to explain how writing this poem had enabled him to discover and better understand the meaning of the limbo dance, often simplified and depoliticised in the touristic exoticising settings in which Caribbean cultures, histories, stories and environments are commodified: 'What I discovered in writing this poem is that in fact it is a strange residual memorial of the slave trade' (Brathwaite 2004, 05:16). With their back facing the floor, the limbo dancer passes under a bar that is gradually lowered, making the movement increasingly challenging. As highlighted by William Harris, limbo is said to have its origins on the slave ships of the Middle Passage across the Atlantic, where the lack of space forced the enslaved people to contort into human spiders. In an article on the subject, the Guyanese intellectual not only acknowledges Kamau Brathwaite's poetic work on the relation between limbo and spider fables, but he quotes the Barbadian poet's text to provide empirical evidence in support of his research and analyses. The scholarly work also examines how Brathwaite's poetry contributes to wider resignifications of the dance and the creation of 'a limbo gateway between Africa and the Caribbean' (Harris 2008, 11). Harris recognises the type of intuitive knowledge that, although not fully articulated with the straightforwardness of some academic literature, arises from the poem in the voice of Caliban. However, it is Brathwaite himself who clearly articulates the main discovery resulting from writing this poem:

> I discovered that the people who are creating or recreating this memorial are also making a very important point: that not only did they suffer the torture of the Middle Passage but that they are able to successfully negotiate that passage, to such a degree, that not only do they go under the stick, but that eventually they rise on the other side of the stick from that position of *nada*, from that position

[4] The Segue Reading Series is an ongoing initiative of The Segue Foundation, a non-profit arts organisation, created and managed by poet James Sherry, supporting the contemporary avant-garde since 1976 (see The Segue Foundation (2024)).

of nothingness, from that position of being absolutely stretched on the floor, they rise like the Sun towards the wonderful glow of the drums, which are waiting for them on the other side. And this is what this poem is trying to do. In fact, this is what I discovered in writing this poem. (Brathwaite 2004, 6:20–7:21)

The discovery illustrated by Brathwaite does not have to do as much with the research process that often accompanies poetry-writing when dealing with either difficult or unknown topics, as with a specific type of *conocimientos* (insights)[5] that are enabled by poetry:

limbo
limbo like me

drum stick knock
and the darkness is over me

knees spread wide
and the water is hiding me

limbo
limbo like me

knees spread wide
and the dark ground is under me

down
down
down

and the drummer is calling me

limbo
limbo like me

sun coming up
and the drummers are praising me

[5] While the noun *conocimiento* often refers to the theory in general, *conocimientos* (in plural) refers to specific findings and insights (see Anzaldúa 2009).

out of the dark
and the dumb gods are raising me
(Brathwaite 1973, 194–5)

I can feel these lines in my body. Fuelled by poetry's own tools, these *conocimientos* are attuned with the *sentipensante* (thinking-feeling) tradition described, practised and further developed, by other subaltern voices from the postcolonial Americas, such as Édouard Glissant (2005; 2010), Gloria Anzaldúa (1987) or, most recently, Cristina Rivera Garza (2022; 2023), who have produced both cultural theory and poetry. *Sentipensar* – to think-feel – is an increasingly used word in decolonising debates (see Escobar 2019; Medina 2021; and Streck 2017). Its origins can be traced back to the early 1980s, through the work of Orlando Fals Borda (1986), who reported its presence in Afro-descendant communities from the Colombian Caribbean coast, where people have used it to express the act of 'thinking from the heart and mind, or co-reasoning' (Botero 2019, 304). As articulated by Arturo Escobar (2020), the idea of *sentipensar* with and within the Earth is a core element of the 'epistemologies from the South' approach to contesting environmental and climate injustice. Brathwaite's readers have access to his profound knowledge of the creative survival and resistance strategies that Africans and Afro-descendants have forged, first, out of the Middle Passage experience across the Atlantic Ocean, and secondly, through the recreation and reinvention of ancestral practices in new American landscapes and seascapes.[6] This *conocimiento socioecológico sentipensante* (thinking-feeling socioecological knowledge) was revealed to the poet through both living and writing.

As a poet-researcher myself, I have experienced the activation of specific parts of my brain, whole body, senses and language, those powerful discovery tools, through writing. Poetry's research tools can help us to understand and to propose innovative approaches, not only to our surroundings, but also to the past, to blind spots in our imperfect intergenerational memory, and therefore, also to the present and our uncertain future. Discovery is, together with a thinking-feeling attitude, movement and transformation, or positive change, at the core of the act of constant research and *poiesis* that is poetry.

---

[6] Rómulo Lachatañeré (1992), in Cuba, and Manuel Zapata Olivella (1989), in Colombia, have studied the survival and resistance cultural practices of African and Afro-descendant peoples who were deprived of their ancestral material culture and environments, as well as their adaptation to and transformation of their new socioecological and spiritual contexts in the Americas.

My poetry, my scholarship

J. Scott Bryson, who had already made a distinction between ecopoetry and conventional lyrical nature poems, in the introduction to the edited collection *Ecopoetry: A critical introduction* (Bryson 2002), has stated that, while ecopoems are indeed simply the latest in a long line of nature poetry, they also are a new type of poem, and part of 'a new movement in poetry, one that seeks to stir readers to action in new ways' (Bryson 2005, 3). Although poets' intentions rarely concern me, due to the belief that a good poem often transcends its author's purposes and reach, I have indeed been moved to academic action – including research and teaching – by both reading and writing poetry.

Writing, performing and critically reading poetry are forms of interaction with the world that not only require but facilitate depth of engagement with diverse human, non-human and more-than-human subject matters. Therefore, these activities can enhance our knowledge of our relations with and within the environment, and could even help us to counteract the negative impact of failed climate communications, which often alienate people from environmental concerns (see Stoknes 2015). Without disregarding the perils of instrumentalising a form of art that is not a mere form of communication, my call to think about our place within the natural world through poetry is aligned with Rosi Braidotti's invitation to assess the human as 'materially embedded and embodied, differential, affective and relational' (Braidotti 2019, 11). This entails looking closer at the material context of subjects, their relations and their diverse lived experiences, while acknowledging the value of subaltern epistemologies, which are still underrepresented in academic discourses that continue to privilege a type of knowledge driven solely by modern rationality. In this light, and in a similar way as palaeoclimatologists employ a wide variety of techniques and interact with ice, pollen, corals or volcanic ash to deduce ancient climates, the poetic subjects in my poems look for answers to the climate crisis through diverse poetic forms, while reflecting upon their relations both within and with the environment.

However, a question remains: why is doubt cast on poetry as a valid form of scholarship? An introduction to the answer could be found in Stephen K. Levine's brief intellectual history of the dispute between poetry and philosophy, in his timely book, *Ecopoiesis: Towards a poietic ecology* (2020). The misconception that art's raw materials are the appearances captured by human senses, is one of the underlying premises of the distinction between philosophy and art, including poetry.

Levine locates the origin, of traditional philosophy's animosity toward art, in Plato, to whom artistic perception and creation, enabled by the senses, did not contribute to true understanding, which is supposed to be based on the unitary essence of immoveable truth. Aristotelian thought continued to consider artistic creation a subordinate form of engagement with reality. 'It is not until Nietzsche that *poiesis* is restored to its central place as our fundamental mode of being and knowing. For Nietzsche, even philosophy is something *made*, and, as such, can be considered art, in spite of its own self-understanding' (Levine 2020; see also Nietzsche 1962). Levine sees Martin Heidegger's phenomenological ontology as a continuation of Nietzsche's fundamental project of restoring *poiesis* to the centre of both human existence and intellectual endeavours. To Heidegger, *poiesis* is a way of knowing intrinsic to mortal beings who live within an historical horizon; therefore, art does not reveal eternal essences, it is rather a work of its time that unveils temporal truths and insights that should evolve both with and for a changing world (see Heidegger 1971).

Heidegger's poetic and philosophical reading of Friedrich Hölderlin's elegy, 'Bread and Wine' (Hölderlin 2022), outlines an answer to the pressing question posed by the poet: '... and what are poets for in a destitute time?' (Hölderlin in Heidegger 1971, 89). Heidegger's answer draws the double role of poetry not only as a form of communication but as research methodology and scholarship: 'The long way leading to the poetry is itself one that inquires poetically' (Heidegger 1971, 94). Furthermore, the philosopher invites us to humbly accept the limits of traditional forms of enquiry, which would include philosophy and literary criticism, and to embrace the slow mode of knowledge-production proposed by poetry:

> We are not only unprepared for an interpretation of the elegies and the sonnets, but also we have no right to it, because the realm in which the dialogue between poetry and thinking goes on can be discovered, reached, and explored in thought only slowly. Who today would presume to claim that he is at home with the nature of poetry as well as with the nature of thinking and, in addition, strong enough to bring the nature of the two into the most extreme discord and so to establish their concord? (Heidegger 1971, 96)

Answers are to continue to be explored both in and through poetry: 'If Rilke is a "poet in a destitute time" then only his poetry answers the question to what end he is a poet, whither his song is bound, where the poet belongs in the destiny of the world's night. That destiny decides what remains fateful within this poetry' (Heidegger 1971, 139). Poetry, as both an applied discipline and a form of scholarship that continues to develop its own methods, is well placed to fill the gap left by traditional humanistic disciplines that have focused mainly on forms of metaliterature and the human experience. With a particular interest in the relations between both sentient and non-sentient components of the environment, poetry, the same as other forms of art, arrived early to the posthuman turn that has crystallised in the so-called new humanities.

My own practice as a researcher would have not advanced in the direction of the environmental humanities without the help of poetry, and my research on hurricane culture, would not exist. The concept of hurricane culture, which I have developed in a monographic book to be published in 2026, refers to the knowledges, beliefs, narratives, practices and artistic expressions acquired and codeveloped over the centuries by diverse peoples who have had to deal with storms and environmental degradation in the Atlantic hurricane belt, a region that includes the northern coast of South America, the Gulf of Mexico, the Antilles, the Lucayan Archipelago and the Florida Peninsula. My book provides comparative cultural analyses of cultural representations of hurricanes, with a focus on the Hispanic Caribbean in relation to other territories of the hurricane belt and the Atlantic coasts of North America and Europe. The proposed analyses highlight the imperative of decolonising socioecological interactions in and between these territories through hurricane culture by historicising vulnerability and resilience. Ultimately, I urge the reader to look at hurricanes as both destructive unnatural extreme weather events accelerated by global warming and as cultural phenomena in nature that connect the peoples and cultures of the hurricane belt and the Atlantic coasts of Africa, North America and Europe. Drawing upon Édouard Glissant's (1997) concept of a 'poetics of relations', I propose to articulate the relational quality of the Atlantic World from an ecocritical perspective, and through an ecopoetics of relations that considers what storms and the environment tell us about our entangled histories and cultures. These ideas and the main research questions for writing my most recent academic book emerged from a single poem, which is included in my unpublished second collection, titled *De corales – Made of Corals* (Jerez Columbié 2024); the English translation is by poet Matthew Geden:

Espejo

antes de caer y hacerse un ovillo
el arrecife tiene dos caras como hoja de yagruma
envoltorio y contenido, negativo y positivo de la imagen, verde y gris
una mirada toda pencas, cielo, alguna nube sobre una capa de plata
una mirada toda agujeros, poros, canales sobre una plancha de vidrio
Huracán también mira de lejos con su único ojo, a veces suspira, se aleja
Huracán brama, irrumpe, baila en su templo con los brazos abiertos, es ritmo y cuchillas
las esponjas de mar licuadas espesan la danza de aletas, pólipos, partículas
se vuelven células buscándose a tientas en la ronda para recomponerse
todos giran, laten, se montan, escupen, se tocan, transmiten, convulsionan
a *jazz* de caja, bombo, toms, goliat, plato *crash, ride, hi hat*
se parten las baquetas, se revientan las cuerdas del violín
se rompe el vidrio, hierve la plata sobre los corales
arrancados de cuajo por el viento y las olas
los animales flotan a la deriva
los animales flotan a la deriva
arrancados de cuajo por el viento y las olas
se rompe el vidrio, hierve la plata sobre los corales
se parten las baquetas, se revientan las cuerdas del violín
a *jazz* de caja, bombo, toms, goliat, plato *crash, ride, hi hat*
todos giran, laten, se montan, escupen, se tocan, transmiten, convulsionan
se vuelven células buscándose a tientas en la ronda para recomponerse
las esponjas de mar licuadas espesan la danza de aletas, pólipos, partículas
Huracán brama, irrumpe, baila en su templo con los brazos abiertos, es ritmo y cuchillas
Huracán también mira de lejos con su único ojo, a veces suspira, se aleja
una mirada toda agujeros, poros, canales sobre una plancha de vidrio

una mirada toda pencas, cielo, alguna nube sobre una capa de plata
envoltorio y contenido, negativo y positivo de la imagen, verde y gris
el arrecife tiene dos caras como hoja de yagruma
antes de caer y hacerse un ovillo

Mirror

before falling and curling up
the reef is two-faced like a yagruma leaf
wrapping and what's inside, negative and positive image, green and grey
a look, all leaves, sky, some cloud on a layer of silver
a look, all holes, pores, channels on a glass plate
Hurricane watches from afar with its one eye, sometimes sighs, walks away
Hurricane roars, bursts, dances on His temple with open arms, rhythm, blades
liquified sea sponges thicken the dance of fins, polyps, particles
they become cells reaching to recompose each other in the round
all turn, beat, ride, spit, touch, transmit, convulse
to the *jazz* of snare, bass drum, toms, goliath, cymbals crash, ride, high hat
the drumsticks snap, violin strings break
glass shatters, silver boils over coral,
uprooted by wind and waves
animals drift
animals drift
uprooted by wind and waves
glass shatters, silver boils over coral,
the drumsticks snap, violin strings break
to the *jazz* of snare, bass drum, toms, goliath, cymbals crash, ride, high hat
all turn, beat, ride, spit, touch, transmit, convulse
they become cells reaching to recompose each other in the round
liquified sea sponges thicken the dance of fins, polyps, particles
Hurricane roars, bursts, dances in His temple with open arms, rhythm, blades
Hurricane watches from afar with its one eye, sometimes sighs, walks away

a look, all holes, pores, channels on a glass plate
a look, all leaves, sky, some cloud on a layer of silver
wrapping and what's inside, negative and positive image, green
  and grey
the reef is two-faced like a yagruma leaf
before falling and curling up

This poem's form is specular, from the Latin *speculum* (mirror). The form was first used by Julia Copus in her 1995 poetry collection *The Shuttered Eye*. The second part of the poem replicates the previous lines in reverse, simultaneously producing a mirroring effect and new meanings. Whereas in Copus's well-known specular poem, 'The Back Seat of My Mother's Car', there is a rear-view mirror, in my poem the effect is supported by the reflecting waters of the Caribbean Sea. My poem also echoes both the sounds and the shape of the so-called annular hurricanes, a symmetrical category of tropical storms, like the ones represented by the Indigenous cultures of the Caribbean (see Knaff et al. 2003; Ortiz 1947). The form of the poem itself, like most of my academic work on cultural theory and the history of ideas, invites the reader to look back, not with the aim of reproducing the past, but to move forward. My poetry is my scholarship, the means to provide my small yet original contribution within and beyond academia and to find and express my own voice, which is a coral one, made of particles and people, from somewhere in West Africa to Guantanamo and Havana, passing through Girona and Cork – and always back to the Caribbean.

References

Anzaldúa, Gloria. 1987. *Borderlands/La Frontera: The new Mestiza*. San Francisco: Aunt Lute Books.

Anzaldúa, Gloria. 2009. *The Gloria Anzaldúa Reader*. Durham, NC: Duke University Press.

Anzaldúa, Gloria. 2015. *Light in the Dark/Luz en lo Oscuro: Rewriting identity, spirituality, reality*. Durham, NC: Duke University Press.

Botero Gómaz, Patricia. 2019. 'Sentipensar'. In *Pluriverse: A post-development dictionary*, edited by Ashish Kothari, Ariel Salleh, Arturo Escobar, Federico Demaria and Alberto Acosta, 302–5. New Delhi: Tulika Books and Authorsupfront.

Braidotti, Rosi. 2019. *Posthuman Knowledge*. Cambridge: Polity Press.

Brathwaite, Kamau. 1973. *The Arrivants: A New World trilogy*. London: Oxford University Press. Accessed 17 July 2025. http://archive.org/details/arrivantsnewworl00brat.

Brathwaite, Kamau. 2004. 'Segue reading at the Bowery Poetry Club, New York City'. Recorded on 1 May 2004. PennSound. Accessed 23 July 2025. https://www.writing.upenn.edu/pennsound/x/Brathwaite.php.

Brathwaite, Kamau. 2005. *Born to Slow Horses*. Middletown, CT: Wesleyan University Press.

Bryson, Scott. 2002. Ecopoetry: A critical introduction. Salt Lake City: University of Utah Press.

Bryson, Scott. 2005. *The West Side of Any Mountain: Place, space, and ecopoetry*. Iowa City: University of Iowa Press.

Cassata, William S. and Paul R. Renne. 2012. 'Fossil raindrops and ancient air', *Nature* 484(7394): 322–4. https://doi.org/10.1038/nature11036.
Cole, David R. 2021. 'The Phallocene'. In *Education, the Anthropocene, and Deleuze/Guattari*, 61–81. Leiden: Brill. https://doi.org/10.1163/9789004505971_004.
Copus, Julia. 1995. *The Shuttered Eye*. Hexham: Bloodaxe Books.
Crutzen, Paul J. and Eugene F. Stoermer. 2000. 'The "Anthropocene"'. In *Paul J. Crutzen and the Anthropocene: A new epoch in Earth's history*, edited by Susanne Benner, Gregor Lax, Paul J. Crutzen, Ulrich Pöschl, Jos Lelieveld and Hans Günter Brauch, 19–21. Cham: Springer International. https://doi.org/10.1007/978-3-030-82202-6_2.
Escobar, Arturo. 2019. 'Thinking-feeling with the Earth: territorial struggles and the ontological dimension of the epistemologies of the South'. In *Knowledges Born in the Struggle: Constructing the epistemologies of the Global South*, edited by Boaventura de Sousa Santos and Maria Meneses, 41–57. Abingdon: Routledge.
Escobar, Arturo. 2020. 'Sentipensar with the Earth: territorial struggles and the ontological dimension of the epistemologies of the South'. In *Pluriversal Politics: The real and the possible*, 67–83. Durham, NC: Duke University Press. https://doi.org/10.1515/9781478012108-008.
Fals Borda, Orlando. 1986. *Retorno a la Tierra: Historia doble de la costa*, vol. 4. Bogotá: Carlos Valencia Editores.
Ferdinand, Malcom. 2019. *Une écologie décoloniale: Penser l'écologie depuis le monde caribéen*. Paris: Éditions du Seuil.
Fortey, Richard A. 2009. *Fossils*. New York: Sterling Publishing.
Geden, Matthew. 2012. *The Place Inside*. Dublin: Dedalus Press.
Geden, Matthew. 2020. *Fruit*. Dublin: SurVision Books.
Geden, Matthew. 2022. *The Cloud Architect*. Connemara, County Galway: Doire Press.
Glissant, Édouard. 1997. *Poetics of Relation*. Ann Arbor: University of Michigan Press.
Glissant, Édouard. 2005. *The Collected Poems of Édouard Glissant*. Minneapolis: University of Minnesota Press.
Glissant, Édouard. 2010 [1969]. *Poetic Intention*. New York: Nightboat Books.
Haraway, Donna. 2015. 'Anthropocene, Capitalocene, Plantationocene, Chthulucene: Making kin', *Environmental Humanities* 6(1): 159–65. https://doi.org/10.1215/22011919-3615934.
Harris, Wilson E. 2008. 'History, fable and myth in the Caribbean and Guianas', *Caribbean Quarterly* 54(1/2): 5–38.
Heidegger, Martin. 1971. 'The origin of the work of art'. In *Poetry, Language, Thought*, 15–86. New York: Harper & Row.
Hölderlin, Friedrich. 2022 [1801]. 'Bread and wine', translated by David Lehman, *Southern Review* 58(4): 637–42. Accessed 17 July 2025. https://muse.jhu.edu/article/865733.
Jerez Columbié, Yairen. 2022. *Fósiles de lluvia*. Madrid: Betania.
Jerez Columbié, Yairen. 2024. *De Corales*. Madrid: Betania.
Knaff, John A., James P. Kossin and Mark DeMaria. 2003. 'Annular hurricanes', *Weather and Forecasting* 18(2): 204–23. https://doi.org/10.1175/1520-0434(2003)018<0204:AH>2.0.CO;2.
Lachatañeré, Rómulo. 1992. *El sistema religioso de los afrocubanos*. Havana: Editorial de Ciencias Sociales.
Levine, Stephen K. 2020. 'Ecopiesis: Towards a poietic ecology'. *Ecopoiesis: Eco-Human Theory and Practice* 1(1): 17–24. https://doi.org/10.24412/2713-184X-2020-1-17-24.
Medina, Néstor. 2021. 'Sentipensando Latina/o/x theoethics', *International Academy of Practical Theology, Conference Series* 2: 98–104. https://doi.org/10.25785/iapt.cs.v2i0.166.
Moore, Jason W. 2016. *Anthropocene or Capitalocene? Nature, history, and the crisis of capitalism*. San Francisco: PM Press.
Nietzsche, Friedrich. 1962. *Thus Spoke Zarathustra*. Baltimore, MD: Penguin Books.
Oliver, Mary. 1995. *Blue Pastures*. Orlando, FL: Harcourt Brace.
Ortiz, Fernando. 1947. *El Huracán Mitología y sus Símbolos*. Mexico City: Fondo de Cultura Económica.
Patel, Raj. 2013. 'Misanthropocene?' *Earth Island Journal*, special issue: 'Manmade: Welcome to the anthropocene' (spring). Accessed 1 April 2025. https://www.earthisland.org/journal/index.php/magazine/entry/misanthropocene.
Rivera Garza, Cristina. 2022. *Escrituras Geológicas*. Madrid: Iberoamericana Vervuert.
Rivera Garza, Cristina. 2023. *Me Llamo Cuerpo que no Está: Poesía completa*. Barcelona: Lumen.

Sánchez, Mikeas. 2024. *How to Be a Good Savage and Other Poems*. Minneapolis, MN: Milkweed Editions.
Segue Foundation. 2024. 'About'. Accessed 1 April 2025. https://www.seguefoundation.com/about.
Shakespeare, William. 2009 [1623]. *The Tempest*. Chennai: Pearson Education India.
Stoknes, Per Espen. 2015. *What We Think About When We Try Not to Think About Global Warming: Toward a new psychology of climate action*. White River Junction, VT: Chelsea Green Publishing.
Streck, Danilo R. 2017. 'Emotions in the history of Latin American popular education: constructions for a thinking-feeling pedagogy'. In *Education and Other Modes of Thinking in Latin America*, edited by Robert Aman and Timothy Ireland, 32–46. London: Routledge.
Zapata Olivella, Manuel. 1989. *Las Claves Mágicas de América*. Barcelona: Plaza & Janés.

2

'Britishness is not Whiteness': youth poets 'bite back' at the education survival complex through a killjoy call-and-response towards creative abolition

Dita N. Love, Debbie Yeboah, Dami Folayan, Shirley May and Princess Arinola Adegbite

> Who gets to write, and not only that: who is read. Whose art is allowed to be valued for public consumption: who makes the allowance, what the allowance is. (Taneja 2022, 61)

Difference without division

On 15 October 2022 a young poet, P. A. Bitez, spoke words of poetry in front of a large crowd gathered at a literary event, Cabaret for Freedom, held inside St John's Church, in Manchester, England. Bitez stood still and poised, speaking with a distinct poetic voice, following in the footsteps of her ancestors, mentors and contemporaries. The first line of her poem resounded through her singing voice: 'for our ancestors and our descendants'. As soon as her singing infilled the church, met with silent reverence from the audience, she began moving with grace, stepped down from the raised stage and walked softly among the narrow passageways cutting through rows of audience members. She spoke:

> Call me Sambo with a cigar
> the daughter who eats Jim Crow for dinner
> the slave who slays the slaver

I formed Empires with my fingers
while they rubbed it in my face
and erased the facts from every page.

Bitez's delivery was skilled balancing protest and rhythmic flow with an emotional intensity that she describes as her 'poetic brand', herself a 'Renaissance arts in human form'. Her poetics radiates through her lines: Black skin is an enigma / they were so afraid of our greatness / so they put us in chains / civilisation my child / even when the West calls me wild'.

Introduced as a 'poem celebrating the majesty, success and resilience of black people through the ages', 'Contemplations' is a poem by P. A. Bitez, the artistic name of poet Princess Arinola Adegbite. With this poem, Princess was among six finalists selected for the BBC's nationwide spoken-word poetry talent competition offering mentorship and a short poetry film from Words First (Adegbite 2021). Princess's poem foregrounds the importance of countering the violent erasure of Black and Afro-diasporic histories, knowledge and creative lineages reclaiming them from anti-Black denial rooted in histories of colonialism and slavery.[1] Centred on Princess's multi-faceted poetics, this chapter explores issues of poetic and educational justice.

The Cabaret for Freedom is held annually at the Manchester Literary Festival, hosted by Young Identity. Young Identity is a Manchester-based combined arts charity and spoken-word poetry collective – endearingly called YI – which showcases homegrown and international poets alongside original poetry by YI's youth members and their mentors. The Cabaret for Freedom events embody YI's mission to work with poetry in all its forms, intersections, and cross-pollination with theatre, performance and music; it celebrates the freedom of creative expression and proudly repudiates stereotypical hierarchies of poetry. YI centres young people's layered identity in a way that sidesteps the

[1] Capital B is often used in reference to Black culture as well as Blackness as a racialised experience, 'to confer respect, signal gravitas, and indicate specificity' (Bruce 2021, 6). Hence, in this project, we capitalise Blackness, Black British and Black radical creativity, with the exception of direct quotes from secondary sources. Our project centres the spoken word's aesthetic kinship with the creative lineages of Black and Afro-diasporic cultures where we see the potential of arts-based Black worldmaking. However, the choice to use a capital B or lowercase b is difficult to understand in isolation. For instance, La Marr Jurelle Bruce intentionally uses lowercase b for 'blackness' that is fluid, collectivist and subversive of Western logics of 'the proper', while at the same time it is 'replete with respect, gravitas, and specificity-in-collectivity, too; its smallness does not limit the infinite care it contains' (Bruce 2021, 6).

pitfalls of identity politics.[2] This means it disrupts the differentiation of poetry into hierarchies of aesthetic value steeped in a social differentiation of poets' cultural identities. Instead, YI refuses to see young lives through stereotypes or deficit, embracing 'difference without separability' (Da Silva 2016).[3]

As part of a partnership between YI and the Poetic Justice Values research project at the University of Cambridge, Princess, an alumna of YI, was commissioned to create an original research-based poem, 'Oral to A4', which drew on her lived experience and the collective voices of YI poets and mentors. This chapter explores 'Oral to A4', a short poetry video filmed in Manchester and hosted online at the spoken-word poetry channel AndWhat TV (Adegbite 2022).[4] In our collaboration we sought to understand young people's sense of poetry and culture, explored alongside their perceptions of Britishness. In part this was driven by the lack of meaningful understanding of spirituality in the context of English schools, which are obliged by educational policy to teach spiritual, moral, social and cultural development (SMSC) alongside fundamental British values across the curriculum, often through humanities subjects like English (Mills 2018). While research on British values is not scarce, research on SMSC largely ceased in the late 1990s and resurfaced contemporarily as pivotal to educational justice/injustice. In this context, this chapter traces Princess's poetic refusal of the violence of the UK's literary and educational establishment, rooted in healing lineages of a Black radical creativity (Bruce 2021; Phalafala 2020; Page and Woodland 2023).

This chapter argues that if poetry, culture and spirituality are to be justice-centred, then there is a need to turn towards radical creative and cultural lineages of Black and Afro-diasporic arts, like spoken-word poetry. Particularly, if poetry and its spiritual potential are to hold meaning in the lives of young people of colour in Britain, then they need to be delinked from embodying unexamined Britishness, synonymous

---

2 For examples of how YI work does not pay lip service to diversity in poetry and demands genuine appreciation of difference as generative of cultural production and literary craft, see their publishing imprint and their anthology series 'No Disclaimers': https://www.youngidentity.org/shop/p/no-disclaimers-volume-two.

3 We see social differentiation as inseparable from poetic hierarchies defined in proximity to Whiteness in the poetic avant-garde. One instance of tokenistic treatment of difference is when poets and their work are prejudicially pigeonholed based on their identity categories, their gender and social location (race, ethnicity, ability, immigration status, socio-economic status, class, sexuality, education).

4 A collaboration with YI arose from an encounter between the two co-authors, Dita and Shirley, at a Cabaret for Freedom event in 2021, following the UK's second nationwide COVID-19 lockdown. This encounter led to a two-year partnership, formed between YI, co-founded by Shirley, the charity's CEO and artistic director, and the Poetic Justice Values research project, started by Dita at the University of Cambridge.

with Whiteness.[5] First, we explore Blackness and Britishness through Manchester-based poet Princess's self-identified lens 'as a Nigerian and Jamaican woman'.[6] Second, we introduce the call-and-response format as a culturally relevant creative critical method. Third, the call-and-response presents spoken-word poetry as a portal to epistemic and aesthetic justice, amid the violence of education that creates unsurvivable conditions for youth of colour and punishes their artistic, cultural and spiritual expression. In conclusion, we gesture towards a generative possibility of practising everyday abolition in the non-formal gathering places of spoken word, where a feminist killjoy poetics (Ahmed 2023) is anti-colonial, anti-carceral and anti-capitalist.

Blackness, Britishness

Britishness is not defined by birthright or citizenship. Rather, it can be defined in terms of national pride, shared understanding, language and commonality in thought. The introduction of British values and their monitoring mechanisms in education systems have increased the politicised nature of the term British. Being Black British is markedly different to being British. Since perceived Britishness is often determined through the lens of racial identity, non-White people within Britain are almost always pushed into the frame of being Brit(ish). Afua Hirsch's

[5] Amid an ongoing debate, among Black studies scholars and professional organisations, on the capitalisation of words to designate people's race, ethnicity and culture, in our project we opted for the capitalisation of both terms, 'Black' and 'White', to indicate the social constructedness of race (Ewing 2020; Sirleaf 2023), with the exception of direct quotations. We use capital 'W' to unsettle 'whiteness as a taken-for-granted social category' (Walker 2021, 61). On the one hand, lowercase 'w' has historically located 'white' as non-racial designation implicated in the embodied normalisation of White supremacy, its pervasiveness in our everyday lives, in the education system and in our cellular experience of the world. On the other, capitalisation of 'White' as a racial category, depending on the context, might be used to reproduce the dominance of Whiteness. Since our project is concerned with the multifaceted regard of language as a liberatory and oppressive tool, we chose to capitalise 'White' as race but we situate this alongside the awareness that unlearning the logics of White body supremacy, as therapist Resmaa Menakem (2021) writes, can only begin within individual bodies and how bodies relate to one another, towards developing collective and sustained embodied trauma-informed anti-racist practices (somatic abolitionism). Our project turned to the arts as a promising site to rehearse the embodiment of creative abolition. Here we centre Menakem's reminder that body-centred practices' capacity for mending racialised trauma are generationally cultivated in Black culture, such as: 'individual and collective humming, rocking, rhythmic clapping, drumming, singing, grounding touch, wailing circles, and call and response' (Menakem 2021, 15).

[6] While Princess's poem dialogues the collective voice of YI youth poets from varied backgrounds, it is outside of the scope of this chapter to focus on the complexity and paramount importance of the experiences of South Asian young people who participated in the workshops and our partnership. We will explore in a different format how the interaction of Blackness and Brownness in the British context is pivotal to debates of teaching SMSC alongside fundamental British values.

aptly titled book, *Brit(ish)* (2018), describes the plight of being Black and British. Black Britishness is perpetually enclosed within a frame of Brit(ish). Since British national identity has formed around a systematic and epistemic erasure, Black people are often only afforded a deferred Brit(ish)ness (Palmer 2020).

This Brit(ish)ness is deferred, or even denied, to Black people, conditioned on the ability to code-switch, be high-achieving and/or contort one's sense of self to align with the aesthetics accepted by Whiteness. Delay or refusal to conform to the norms of Whiteness is further suppressed into existence in the 'othered' basement of society. Blackness inhibits acceptance as British, due to 'whiteness being axiomatic of Englishness' (Gilroy 2013 cited by Madriaga and McCaig 2022, 85). This social reality is not reflective of legal realities since, as outlined by Hansen (1999, 94, cited by Campt 2017, 29), 'Those arriving from the colonies and independent Commonwealth countries landed in the UK as citizens. From a strictly legal point of view, the term "commonwealth immigrant" is a misnomer; Commonwealth immigrants were citizens exercising the rights of citizenship'.

Despite the growing body of literature on the experiences of Black people, there is still little consensus on what it means to be Black. Maylor's (2014) paper, 'What is the meaning of "black"? Researching "black" participants', makes a significant contribution to our understanding of Blackness through a study on self-identification. Maylor (2014, 369) highlights the term Black as a political signifier, which has 'at times been used to identify those who experience structural and institutional discrimination because of their skin colour'. Through this positioning of the term Black, Maylor (2014) emphasises the collective employment of Black as a positioning term that enforces a sense of comradery and kinship in response to collective sufferings. In the UK, Black historically referred to anyone who is not White, encompassing people of African, Caribbean, Asian and Latin American descent. The collective commitment to the term Black was most prevalent in 1960s and 1980s Britain (Maylor 2014). Since that time, however, classification categories have shifted, reorganising and reconstructing the term Black.[7] Changes to the 2001 census saw a 'move towards "pan-ethnic" groups'.[8] Hence, census categories can be noted to have formalised a cultural division that

[7] Our partnership was a site where young people spoke of the vital importance of connecting across cultural groups, particularly between Black British and South Asian communities, in the context of perceptions of Britishness which we plan to elucidate in the future.

[8] The census categories included 'White', 'Mixed', 'Asian or Asian British', 'Black or Black British', and 'Chinese or Other Ethnic Group' (Aspinall 2002, 804). This differed from the 1991 census,

occurred as a result of the differentiation in suffering that was evident between Afro-Caribbean and Asian communities within the UK.

The changes to the use of the term Black highlight the term's fluidity. Despite the fluidity that can be seen through historic uses of Black, the term maintains 'a precise meaning when used by individuals as a "self-identifier", [and] becomes "imprecise" when "used as a collective term for groups perceived to share some common ethnic attributes"' (Aspinall 2022, 810).[9] Through our engagement with Blackness and Britishness, we emphasise the fluidity of identity and our belief that identity is not stasis or a point of arrival, but rather a process of becoming (Hall 2015). We explore tensions associated with being and becoming British in relation to justice-centred poetry.

Culturally relevant creative critical enquiry

Our creative critical enquiry turns to culturally relevant poetry-based methodologies, specifically the format of the call-and-response in which we combine Princess's voice as a call and our collective response in a plural voice (Glynn 2019).[10] The context was a two-year-long partnership between the Poetic Justice Values project and YI, which was an interface to explore in action what an anti-oppressive design might look like for creative community and university collaborations (Benjamin 2019). We delivered three workshops, with up to 20 young people facilitated by guest poet educators, working across poetry, hip hop, mixed performing arts and grime poetry.[11] This culminated in the Going Places conference inspired by the poetry of British poet Lemn Sissay who opened the conference alongside YI poets, Princess Arinola Adegbite, aka P. A. Bitez, Safwat Elsenossi, aka SAF-S2E and Maya Chowdhury, at the University of Cambridge (Love et al. 2024). At the conference, we also held a workshop with the YI leadership team, where

---

which featured groupings of 'White', 'Black-Caribbean', 'Black-African', 'Black-Other', 'Indian', 'Pakistani', 'Bangladeshi' and 'Chinese' (Jivraj 2012). Prior to 1991, the UK census did not capture information about racial identity.

[9] The limits of self-identifier here do not apply in instances of appropriation and abuse of Black culture, such as White people claiming African-American heritage and identity, as Princess's poem 'Contemplations' calls out subtly and sardonically, in her line 'Rachel Dolezal's icon'.

[10] Our use of the group pronoun 'we' neither homogenises nor relativises.

[11] The partnership and its lessons will be discussed on another occasion. The three guest facilitators we worked with were: Suhaiymah Manzoor-Khan, author of *Postcolonial Banter*, and *Tangled in Terror: Uprooting Islamophobia*; BREIS, founder of Student of Life, a hip hop inspired arts organisation, author of *Brilliant Rappers Educate Intelligent Students* and *Diary of a Creative Mind*; and Deborah 'Debris' Stevenson, author of acclaimed debut play, *Poet in da Corner*.

we deepened our enquiry of YI's practice. YI's work stands out for the quality of its literary teaching, visual identity and multimedia poetry creation; its educational ethos uplifts young people 'at risk of being excellent', modelling trust, not tokenism. Its mentors work alongside and with youth artists, where mentorship is cross-generational, mutual and banishes youth saviourism.

Our employment of call-and-response stems from our theoretical turn to Black Studies and Black feminist scholarship. Davis (2021) highlights that call-and-response is intrinsic to many Black cultures, noting that critical poetic enquiry as a methodology presents call-and-response in research. Our turn to call-and-response is a kind of response in itself to Davis's (2021, 122) call, to advance the methodological framework of critical poetic enquiry through engagement and to 'strengthen the collective work'.[12] In this way, this chapter does not just employ a method and analytic of call-and-response but operates in response to multiple calls, including the YI poets' collective call captured in Princess's poem. Through this paper, we move beyond the dichotomy of creative works and academic argumentation, seeing poetry as 'valid as academic writing' (Davis and McTier 2023, 763).

The call-and-response is attuned to the theorisation of the cut, by Black studies scholar James Snead (1981). The cut is a place of beauty, creation and recreation, which allows the semblances of music, performance and reality to be recognised, as we circle and cut back to moments that we have already seen, through the eyes of those who have gone before us, but are never quite able to relive, in the newly contoured context of our realities. The cuts found in the rhythmic figures of life remind us that 'what has been will be again, what has been done will be done again; there is nothing new under the sun' (*Bible*, Ecclesiastes 1:9). Snead elaborated the 'magic of the cut' in Black culture as 'cultural coverage'; as generatively subversive by making known anomalies as possibilities that can be transformative within systems (Snead 1981, 652). We are curious about the poetics of the 'cut', for its capacities of making manifest worlds outside of systems of oppression.

Poetic enquiry informs our creative critical method approach, for it not only centres minoritised voices, but acts as an entryway for minoritised scholars, as noted by Davis (2021, 114), to 'protest dominant,

[12] The scholar and poet Camea Davis, together with Syreeta Ali McTier, introduced their poetic call-and-response methodology and paper as part of a series of webinars and workshops under the banner of Creative Critical Methods For(u)m, organised by first author Dita at the University of Cambridge. The recorded webinar video was an instructive resource shared with the co-authors of this chapter, which we revisited in the writing process.

Eurocentric epistemologies, research texts, and societal injustices'. We engage in interdisciplinary work that breaks from conventional academic writing (Sandal-Wilson and Tanna 2020) and the constructedness of socioscientific knowledge, often concealed through academic prose (Richardson 1993, cited by Zaino and Bell 2022). Poetic enquiry assembles text and language to excavate the nonverbal, the somatic truth and the wisdom of the body; it can unlock liminal and implicit knowledge without which commitments to justice cannot reckon with present legacies of collective traumas. As such, we centre this method as culturally relevant and attuned to our affiliation with Black abolitionist and killjoy feminist scholarship, infused as a citational practice in the call-and-response section.

As co-authors of this chapter, we come together in our shared interests as artists, poets, educators and wilful scholars (Ahmed 2017). Princess is a writer, spoken-word poet, musician, actress and filmmaker from Manchester, and alumna of YI, where she was mentored by Shirley during the production of 'Oral to A4'. Shirley is a poet and the director of YI, who has worked for 18 years to promote a culture around performance poetry and supporting new writers in schools. Dita connected to Shirley and YI after working and living in Manchester. Dita is a White South-Eastern European poet, researcher and educator from an Aromanian ethnic background, which has partly shaped her work with creative critical youth interventions and education, contemporary intergenre poetry and healing intergenerational social justice. Debbie is a Ghanaian artist, educator and researcher utilising contemporary African artwork as a pedagogical pathway towards decolonisation of curricula. Together with Dita, Debbie co-convened the Going Places conference and cochaired the roundtable discussion with the YI poets. Dami is a Christian Black-British woman poet, theorist and sociologist of education. Dami spoke to YI poets at one of our workshops, sharing her research with critical poetic enquiry on widening access and looking at the experiences of Black women at Oxbridge.

We attempt to work with and against the paradox of feminist positionality (Georgiann and Khonach 2020). In Ahmed's words: '*Strangerwise* is an odd word for an old wisdom, the wisdom of strangers, those who, in being estranged from worlds, notice them' (Ahmed 2023, 178). We understand strangerwise as a positionality that affords anti-oppressive feminist ways of knowing, being and writing. We claim opacity to our positionality, while seeking 'killjoy truths' (Ahmed 2023, 196) for our feminist accountability. Opacity does not sacrifice rigour, it is a way of becoming undisciplined in all the ways institutionalised rigour disciplines our bodies, hearts and minds (Owusu 2025). This means that feminist positionality can become 'a kind of estrangement from the world and thus involves moments of self-estrangement. Our feminist archive is an archive of unhappiness [with oppression] even though the threads of unhappiness do not weave our stories together' (Ahmed 2020, 86).[13] Thus, the call-and-response structure serves not just as a methodological tool but as a profound means of revisiting, exploring and relating to Princess's poetics, presented in the next section.

Killjoy call-and-response

Driven by the themes of Princess's poem, 'Oral to A4', the roundtable conversation began with reflections on epistemic violence (Dotson 2011; Spivak 1988) of British (European) curricula. Epistemic violence is here understood as the complex power of interlocking systems of oppression that have worked to silence and erase the legitimacy of knowledge and histories of people of colour. Princess's poem melds edifying insights into the hegemony of Western poetry with clever exposition of the domination of the literary canon, as it is taught in English schools. To counter epistemic violence, the conversation became a frank exercise of the generative possibilities of epistemic, aesthetic and spiritual disobedience (Mignolo 2009; Weidler 2020; Ahsan and Williams 2022), led by the youth poets. The dialogue ensued, centring 'Oral to A4' as a portal for delinking the lived experience of the colonised curriculum from the tradition of the spoken word as more than an art form performed live to an audience. Spoken word lifts off the page, lyrically liberated and unconstrained by Eurocentric written form. The spoken centred pluriversal concerns of those who have often been marginalised. This conversation was an implicit exploration of anti-colonial arts praxis, in which young people harness poetry within both communal and individual spaces. The conversation offered a thoughtful provocation to forms of violence and gatekeeping that shape artistic expression and reception: the colonial

[13] We refuse the notion of transparent disclosure of authors' identities, as part of positionality, as we refuse to either over-justify our scholarly place or parade biographical details, which are disproportionately expected and demanded as defence of rigour from writers and scholars who have been multiply marginalised. Who and what can be recognised as a stranger, as not belonging, might include individuals or groups as well as categories of identity and social location from gender, race, class, sexuality, ability, ethnicity, immigration status and education. Strangerwise positionality can be an act of feminist self-preservation, not self-effacement.

legacies and reduction of Black imagination, the anti-Black violence of education and the criminalisation of Black art, that persist in society and education systems.

Call: In the worlding of the word, whose truths are deemed worthy of worship?

Our first call arises through the stanzas from 'Oral to A4' that probe into the hypocrisy of the 'avant-garde' within the contemporary poetry scene, which unfolds unexamined elitist and racist legacies:

> Google greatest poets,
>
> It'll rarely show ethnic or working-class bards,
> Though we remain the definition of Avant Garde.
> Serving Sage like Suhaiymah, zealous like Zephaniah,
> We can pen iambic pentameter, but we'd rather write bars.
>
> We the renaissance to resurrect light from the dark
> For in the beginning, there was only the word.
> We're too hypnotic to ever follow the herd,
> Flip the script of A4, remember the spoken was first.

As a poet, Princess said: 'I am trying to be my own icon. Everything I write I try to make it emotionally intense. My brand is actually intensity. I always keep my eye out for hypocrisy from people who don't want change'. 'Oral to A4' was filmed on location at Manchester's Portico Library, which has a colonial history. Princess said: 'The library has a lot of rich literature, but literature that if I was alive back then, I wouldn't be considered human, I wouldn't be considered an artist, I wouldn't be considered having a brain to create'. This recalls La Marr Jurelle Bruce's (2021, 4) perspicuous account of Black radical creativity, madness and resistance: 'The Middle Passage literally deranged and threw millions of Africans askew across continents, oceans, centuries, and worlds. I use derange also to signal how the Atlantic slave trade, and the anti-Black modernity it inaugurated, framed Black people as always already wild, subrational, pathological, mentally unsound, mad.' Cognisant of these anti-Black legacies, Princess stated how the conceptual filmmaking decisions contributed to a wilfulness to 'bite back' at the racist dehumanisation of Black people.[14] The film's juxtaposition of reading from a physical book to speaking words by heart embodied the ambivalence writers feel through the imposed dominance of the written over the spoken word. Princess said that in the poetry film she spoke the concluding poetry lines 'looking at the camera only, being firmly rooted in my spoken-word heritage and my oral tradition heritage as a Nigerian and Jamaican woman, that is how my stories and histories were told'.

Response

Our truths *are* worthy. Period. Poetry, is rebellion, it is refusal. It defies normativity. It questions, it challenges, it delinks, it dismantles. With verse, we wrench at the binding of societal constructs that loom large over our lives. Poetry wields power to perceive, to expose the fissures in Eurocentric paradigms, revealing the spaces we crack open, the spaces become sites of resistance. Through every stanza, and each uttered word, we poets reclaim the narratives, transforming the act of expression into a portal for societal transformation. No more reliance on English literature for reformation, there is only reimprisoning in its bars. Reformation comes through revelation, and revelation through the spoken word at the end of the world as new beginning. Our spoken poetry is not just art form made audible, but a mosaic where humanness and the multiverse of experiences refract differences without division which constitute our collective realities. It is evidence of our felt theorisation that, in the cacophony of life, every murmur holds the weight of worlds. We yearn to arrange these worlds otherwise. We are moved to question our complicity with institutionalised artistic norms that create unsurvivable conditions for our words, our worlds.[15]

We heard that '[to] encounter the history of avant-garde poetry is to encounter a racist tradition' (Hong 2020). We encounter Princess's

[14] The verb 'bite back' was introduced by Princess Arinola Adegbite and alludes to the anti-colonial act of writing back to Empire and centring the spoken-word poetry alongside other Afro-diasporic art forms as formative of many worldwide poetic ecologies. It is also an allusion to her surname Adegbite and artistic name Bitez.

[15] Aesthetic disobedience is used in relation to Princess's killjoy poetics as a radical and anti-colonial worldmaking project. Aesthetic disobedience has been elaborated in relation to civil disobedience in public art projects (Neufeld 2015); and in relation to participatory arts as an 'artistic arrangement for imparting dissident desire' (Weidler 2020, 458) after Kristeva's proposal for mobilising 'art-induced psychosis as a gateway to social reform' (Weidler 2020, 463). The former contributes to disruption of received norms of artistry and its socio-political bounds. The latter accentuates the dissident figure of the artist (after Julia Kristeva) to distribute affective attachments to hegemonic conditions (after Sara Ahmed) towards social change via art and activism (artivism).

killjoy poetics as untethered to the racialised bordering of radical Black creativity. We sense how 'orality should not only exist within world literature, to cure elitist postcolonial school of thoughts that reproduce epistemicide, but is also key in the decolonial imperative of epistemic justice' (Phalafala 2020, 195). We listen to Princess's affirmation of lineages: 'Griot traditions ushered our current MCs and Rappers'. In them we encounter expansive art-making through the sovereignty of aurality and storytelling which does not sacrifice the radical impulse of a killjoy poetics.[16] We see the avant-garde as a killjoy poetics – anti-colonial, anti-carceral and anti-capitalist in the same breath. It is a fresh breath of art-making that insists on worlding for 'There is poetry in killing joy, a rearranging of worlds as well as words, breathing life into arrangements' (Ahmed 2023, 177).

Call: Who gets to decide what is lowbrow and high art? Who decides whose voices and movements resound through the ivory tower and beyond?

Our second call is assembled from Princess's subversion of the hegemonic worship of poetry only when it approximates Whiteness. Princess said that she wanted to reclaim and reaffirm spoken-word lineages and legacies by 'protesting the subtle ways people are indoctrinated into pedestaling certain artforms and artists over others'. She pointed to hypocrisies within the art world, within society, and a colonial tradition, which have shaped 'how Black art and working-class art are perceived on the outskirts'. For example, she evoked American rapper Tupac Shakur as 'inherently poetic', but like rap, spoken word 'is often not taken seriously'. She noted the ramification of racialised hierarchies in the educational exclusion of marginalised aspiring youth poets 'who never got the chance to be poets because they were maligned by a teacher in school and they believe that teacher'. Hence, Princess's stanzas bite back at the oppression of education systems and the poetic canon:

> Brains – naked blank pages of A4,
> Our Shakespeare was Tupac Shakur,
> Sitting at the edge of English class
> Taught the noble savage, magic moor. [...]

[16] Griots are West African public poet figures, orators and storytellers.

Spoken word has enough clout to make you clap your hands
And click your fingers yet the establishment
Only grant honours to Sonnets, Tankas and Sestinas,
Archaic anchors to pseudo grandeur.

Who gets to decide what is low-brow and high-brow art?
They got it wrong with Kusama, Bukowski and Basquiat
Unseen syllabus, whitewashed propaganda not unlike swastikas,
Still no lessons on text being an invention of Mesopotamia.

Response

In both the quietude of thought and the clamour of discourse, our answer is found in the convergence around the word. Decolonisation is not merely the act of diversifying shelves but a profound reclamation of narrative sovereignty. In the classroom, we have a right to hear our stories expressed, like breath, our voices accumulate. As we create afresh, an assemblage of voices that intone from the bounds of liminality, resonant with the depth of untold stories, now finding space, expanding out into the archives of knowledge. In this space, our hearts are emboldened. Here poetry makes manifold meaning, all pluriversal. We have epistemic agency. We are legible as knowers. It is through collaboration that we confront the legacies that sought to silence, and erase, crafting instead a refrain that rises outside of the vestiges of empire, in spite of exclusionary poetic canons. The feminist writer Sara Ahmed, evoking poet Claudia Rankine writes: 'Poetry as high culture is deemed to come from higher people, from white people. There can be a hierarchy to suffering' (Ahmed 2023, 176). Spoken-word poetry is embraced as aesthetic kin of 'Black radical traditions where "radical" is located in resistance against the unworlding of the world' (Phalafala 2020, 195). Hence, Princess's poetics has worldmaking aspirations.

As feminist writer Sara Ahmed writes: 'some of the work we do as feminist killjoys in giving problems their names could be understood as poetry […] A killjoy rearrangement of the past brings us closer to the truth, **killjoy truths**' (Ahmed 2023, 196, emphasis original). We recognise the education survival complex as an unnamed problem in England not dissimilar from the unacknowledged scale of its problem of racism in Britain. Abolitionist educator and scholar Bettina Love, uses the term 'educational survival complex' for 'an educational system built on the suffering of students of colour', in which 'students are left learning to merely survive, learning how schools mimic the world they live in, thus making schools a training site for a life of exhaustion' (Love 2019, 30). Systems invested in the logics of colonial racial capitalism enable the accumulation of dark suffering and lead to spirit-murder and premature death of Black and Brown people (Love 2019; Gilmore 2022; Koshy et al. 2022).[17]

Call: Whose spirits, dreams and faiths can go unpunished, beyond surviving towards thriving in and outside bars and institutional walls?

Our third call arises from our understanding of Princess's killjoy poetics as an abolitionist critique of the education survival complex and the racialised criminalisation of Black artists. Black artists are prosecuted and imprisoned through the use of their rap lyrics in UK courts (Oliver 2023).[18] Princess stressed the hypocrisy when judges prescribe Jane Austen novels to rehabilitate a White man expressing violent thoughts like school bombing, while the lyrics of Black artists, predominately men, are used as criminal evidence to punish and imprison. She said: 'our imagination is not like White men, it is reduced. It is like we can't have imagination, exactly what we say is what we are, there's no space for nuances'. Princess traced the seemingly subtle links between criminalisation of language and the violence of language in the English classroom. She reminisced how teachers spoke the N word in class, saying it was contextual and relevant to the books read. While Princess was interested in reading the books in class, she explained: 'you can just say "the N word", not the actual word, you don't need to be *that* specific'. The educational survival complex is linked to the prison industrial complex through the school-to-prison pipeline and the carcerality of both systems, which profit from the unjust policing of students of colour, often under the guise of security, order and safeguarding. Here we evoke the words of Black studies scholar Saidiya Hartman (2020)

[17] Princess's poetics served as a way to detect disparate forms of veiled violences of coloniality, racism and carcerality reproduced across poetic circles, the education system and society at large, which we recognise as the fabric of colonial racial capitalism. The analytic lens of colonial racial capitalism links 'logics and violences of domination and dispossession to interconnections among colonialism, racial capitalism, and formations of social difference' (Koshy et al. 2022, 7).
[18] Princess spoke eloquently on the real-life ramifications of the criminalisation of drill. The UK campaign Art not Evidence is working to stop the use of rap lyrics in criminal court proceedings.

who said: ‘policing the imagination is the work of oppression’, offering Princess’s stanzas:

> Same courts that use lyrics to convict Drill poets sentence
> White supremacists to read English Literature classics
> Like racists weren’t taught Pride and prejudice
> In books and on blackboards, Mice and Men and
> Teachers so called contextual uses of the N word.
>
> In high school I was always put on behavioural report
> Straight A student scarlet letter for my so called back talk.
> Forced to absorb, cram, and conform, scored on my ability
> To cite texts from a secondary source.

Response

Between the lines of the debate on lowbrow and high art, and the criminalisation of rap lyrics, we read: the war on youth; a spirit-murder, four hundred years in the making through the ongoing war on Blackness (Farr 2022; The Poet 2024). The war on Blackness inheres in the potency of White supremacist control over determining the stories and language used to describe Black lived experiences.[19] The war on Blackness is not a metaphor, and White privilege is ‘the ability to stay alive’ (Hirsch 2020). Here we invoke the figure of the abolitionist killjoy (Dilts 2021; Davis 2011; Gilmore 2022).[20] The abolitionist killjoy seeks to dismantle and rebuild otherwise the intolerable conditions of carcerality, its logics of punishment and governance of bodies seen as other. We cannot choose ignorance over killjoying the normalisation of White profit from the anti-Black institutional confinement of minoritised groups be it a prison cell, a hospital ward or school detention. ‘In becoming a killjoy, becoming a problem as a practice of active intolerance of the

[19] This passage recognises the murder of George Floyd by a White police officer as a continuation of the historical four-hundred-year-old war on Blackness which has been denied and masked by dominant narratives across socio-economic, religious and political spheres.

[20] We invoke the figure of the abolitionist killjoy in relation to the carcerality of the system of education and its links to the criminal justice system. Originally, the abolitionist killjoy was proposed by Andrew Dilts, who elaborates their role in discerning the harms of imprisonment after the abolition feminist stance that prisons are never not punitive and cannot be reformed, they are obsolete. Dilts’ abolitionist killjoy draws on Sara Ahmed’s study of the distribution of affects and affective attachments. We also acknowledge Sara Ahmed’s account of the feminist killjoy as an activist who turns to prison abolition as the indispensable horizon for feminist killjoy justice.

intolerable, one can redistribute negative affect in ultimate service of abolishing the intolerable. We can become abolitionist killjoys' (Dilts 2021, 639).

There is a disavowal of the spiritual in young lives and a hostility to the idea of God inhabiting the hearts, minds and bodies of people of colour, for it is often policed and equated with terror (a la Prevent[21]). In particular, faith and spiritual practice becomes a threat to Western civilisation and its preservation of reason above all, in apparent juxtaposition to the origins of the colonial project, where faith became a vessel through which colonialism was delivered. In the contemporary moment, faith is often seen as in opposition to rationality, and epistemic agency (Dotson 2011). Youth poets harness their poems to explore existential questions, personal beliefs and the divine. In the sacred echo of the verse, faith in self and the spiritual finds its expression, surpassing the confines of belief to touch all who listen, sense, feel, see, move, read – across all faiths and none. Within the lilts of faith-infused poetry, our spiritual quests, though varied, share a common yearning to go beyond speaking back to power, and meet across (sonic) colour lines of power and privilege (Stoever 2016). In the love of life, God, inheritances, artistic kinship and social causes we cocreate making our presence discernible in everyday life.

Gesturing towards creative abolition

This chapter explored how youth poets define the avant-garde on their own terms, outside of Britishness synonymous with Whiteness, through the example of the poem by Princess Arinola Adegbite, an alumna of the Manchester-based arts charity and spoken-word collective Young Identity (YI). Through the collaborative work with Princess and YI as part of the Poetic Justice Values project, the chapter presented youth poets' views of spoken-word poetry as an anti-colonial arts praxis. By engaging with themes of identity beyond identity politics, spirituality and resistance, youth poets demonstrated their ability to uncover the transformative potential of spoken-word poetry to challenge, heal and inspire others who feel the constraints of the poetic forms encountered in the Western canon (Davis 2018). As co-authors, poets, educators and researchers, we presented a collective call-and-response as vehicle of our insights from Princess's poem and youth poets' roundtable discussion.

[21] UK government-led, multi-agency programme aiming to stop individuals becoming terrorists.

We experimented with a culturally relevant method reflective of youth poets' wilfulness to interrogate societal and literary norms conceived as a killjoy poetics aimed at dismantling the anti-Black colonial and carceral violence from the poetry scene and school classroom through the prison pipeline. Our response was an offering and conversation with, by and for young poets and academics, towards meeting youth as space makers who bridge the two. Through revisiting our collaboration in a call-and-response format, we clarified our seeing of poetry where it is often unseen, in communal spaces as its own critical intervention. While there is ambivalence about writing and performing poetry, different formats of coming together reflect different poetic traditions. This experiment of delinking from institutionalised rigour in our writing hoped to reflect youth poets' resistance against the conventional norms of poetry learning, centring spoken word as generative of worldwide poetic traditions and new forms. We saw youth dreams of the avant-garde as spiritual, cultural, embodied, inherited, spoken, aurally sovereign, Black-skin-loving, enfleshed wisdom, as beats and bars, as the magic 'cut' of cultural worlding of a world yet to come, a world that is already here. Youth poets undiscipline poetry as we know it, and in this we turn to 'discipline our hopes' for justice (Kaba 2021). It is not that we ignore the violence of the British educational survival complex that profits from Black and Brown suffering, it is that in the material presence of youth poets' spoken words we are emboldened to see beyond the war on youth of colour through the looking glass of colonial racial capitalism. In so doing, illustrating the potency of spoken poetry as a portal, killjoy truths and communal healing become a promise beyond survival (Gumbs 2025). We seek accountability in our commitments to connect our everyday ways of being and relating (Lamble 2021), recalling complicity and abolitionist lineages of social and creative movements of collective liberation, for in wherever the spoken is remembered as first, we feel beckoned to be present with and for one another.

References

Adegbite, Princess Arinola. 2021. 'P. A. Bitez – Contemplations'. BBC, 21 April. Accessed 19 July 2025. https://www.bbc.co.uk/programmes/p09d0h08.

Adegbite, Princess Arinola. 2022. 'Oral to A4'. AndWhat TV, Manchester, 24 August. Accessed 19 July 2025. https://www.youtube.com/watch?v=36D0HJFceQM.

Ahmed, Sara. 2017. *Living a Feminist Life*. Durham, NC: Duke University Press.

Ahmed, Sara. 2020. 'Feminist killjoys'. In *The Promise of Happiness*, 50–87. Durham, NC: Duke University Press.

Ahmed, Sara. 2023. 'The feminist killjoy as poet'. In *The Feminist Killjoy Handbook*: *The radical potential of getting in the way*, 159–96. London: Allen Lane.

Ahsan, Sanah and Emma Williams. 2022. '"We are creating conditions for young people that are un-survivable": An interview with Sanah Ahsan', *Journal of Philosophy of Education* 56: 88–93.
Aspinall, Peter J. 2002 'Collective terminology to describe the minority ethnic population: The persistence of confusion and ambiguity in usage', *Sociology* 36(4): 803–16.
Benjamin, Ruha. 2019. 'Introduction: Discriminatory design, liberating imagination'. In *Captivating Technology: Race, carceral technoscience, and liberatory imagination in everyday life*, 1–22. Durham, NC: Duke University Press.
Bible. 2011. *New International Version*, Ecclesiastes 1:9. London: Hodder & Stoughton.
Bruce, La Marr Jurelle. 2021. *How to Go Mad without Losing Your Mind: Madness and black radical creativity*. Durham, NC: Duke University Press.
Campt, Tina M. 2017. *Listening to Images*. Durham, NC: Duke University Press.
Da Silva, Denise Ferreira. 2016. 'On difference without separability'. In *32nd Bienal de São Paulo: Incerteza viva. Catalogue*, 57–65. São Paulo: Fundação São Paulo. Accessed 7 October 2025. https://issuu.com/bienal/docs/32bsp-catalogo-web-en.
Davis, Angela Y. 2011. *Are Prisons Obsolete?* New York: Seven Stories Press.
Davis, Camea. 2018. 'Writing the self: Slam poetry, youth identity, and critical poetic inquiry', *Art/Research International: A transdisciplinary journal* 3(1): 90–113.
Davis, Camea. 2021. 'Sampling poetry, pedagogy, and protest to build methodology: Critical poetic inquiry as culturally relevant method', *Qualitative Inquiry* 27(1): 114–24.
Davis, Camea and Syreeta Ali McTier. 2023. 'A call and response critical poetic inquiry of resistance ideologies among teachers and Black youth', *International Journal of Qualitative Studies in Education* 36(5): 759–73.
Davis, Georgiann and Torisha Khonach. 2020. 'The paradox of positionality: Avoiding, embracing, or resisting feminist accountability', *Fat Studies* 9: 101–13.
Dilts, Andrew. 2021. 'How does it feel to be(come) a problem? Active intolerance and the abolitionist killjoy', *Theory & Event* 24: 637–43.
Dotson, Kristie. 2011. 'Tracking epistemic violence, tracking practices of silencing', *Hypatia* 26: 236–57.
Ewing, Eve L. 2020. 'I'm a Black scholar who studies race. Here's why I capitalize "White"'. *Zora*. Accessed 7 October 2025. https://zora.medium.com/im-a-black-scholar-who-studies-race-here-s-why-i-capitalize-white-f94883aa2dd3.
Farr, Arnold L. 2022. 'The War on Blackness: Black men and the state of the union'. In *Black Men from Behind the Veil: Ontological interrogations*, edited by George Yancy, 49–59. London: Rowman & Littlefield.
Gilmore, Ruth Wilson. 2022. 'Abolition geography and the problem of innocence'. In *Abolition Geography: Essays towards liberation*, 471–96. London: Verso Books.
Gilroy, Paul. 2013. *There Ain't No Black in the Union Jack*. Abingdon: Routledge.
Glynn, Martin. 2019. *Speaking Data and Telling Stories: Data verbalization for researchers*. Abingdon: Routledge.
Gumbs, Alexis Pauline. 2025. *Survival Is a Promise: The eternal life of Audre Lorde*. London: Penguin Random House.
Hall, Stuart. 2015. 'Cultural identity and diaspora'. In *Colonial Discourse and Post-Colonial Theory*, edited by Patrick Williams and Laura Chrisman, 392–403. Abingdon: Routledge.
Hansen, Randall. 1999. 'The politics of citizenship in 1940s Britain: The British Nationality Act', *Twentieth Century British History* 10: 67–95.
Hartman, Saidiya. 2020. 'Under the blacklight. Storytelling while Black and female: conjuring beautiful experiments'. Series talk, African-American Policy Forum. Accessed 19 July 2025. https://www.youtube.com/watch?v=xGS5aP5Vi7g.
Hirsch, Afua. 2018. *Brit(ish): On race, identity and belonging*. London: Vintage.
Hirsch, Afua. 2020. 'Claudia Rankine: "By white privilege I mean the ability to stay alive"'. *The Guardian*, 7 September. Accessed 19 July 2025. https://www.theguardian.com/books/2020/sep/05/claudia-rankine-by-white-privilege-i-mean-the-ability-to-stay-alive.
Hong, Cathy Park. 2014. 'Delusions of whiteness in the avant-garde', *Lana Turner* 7. Accessed 7 October 2025. https://shc.stanford.edu/arcade/interventions/delusions-whiteness-avant-garde.
Jivraj, Stephen. 2012. 'Modelling socioeconomic neighbourhood change due to internal migration in England', *Urban Studies* 49(16): 3565–78.

Kaba, Mariame. 2021. *We Do This 'Til We Free Us: Abolitionist organizing and transforming justice*. Chicago: Haymarket Books.

Koshy, Susan, Lisa Marie Cacho, Jodi A. Byrd and Brian Jordan Jefferson. 2022. 'Introduction'. In *Colonial Racial Capitalism*, edited by Susan Koshy, Lisa Marie Cacho, Jodi A. Byrd and Brian Jordan Jefferson, 1–33. Durham, NC: Duke University Press.

Lamble, Sarah. 2021. 'Practising everyday abolition'. In *Abolishing the Police*, edited by Koshka Duff, 147–60. London: Dog Section Press.

Love, Bettina L. 2019. *We Want to Do More than Survive: Abolitionist teaching and the pursuit of educational freedom*. Boston: Beacon Press.

Love, Dita N., Shirley May, Safwat Elsenosi and Dami Folayan. 2024. '"Respect is a recurring choice": Award-winning poet SAF-S2E reflects on the burdened integrity of artistry' [blog post], *Cambridge Digital Humanities*, 3 April.

Madriaga, Manuel and Colin McCaig. 2022. 'How international students of colour become Black: A story of whiteness in English higher education', *Teaching in Higher Education* 27(1): 84–98.

Maylor, Uvanney. 2014. 'What is the meaning of "black"? Researching "black" respondents'. In *Gender, Race and Religion*, edited by Martin Bulmer and John Solomos, 155–73. London: Routledge.

Menakem, Resmaa. 2021. *My Grandmother's Hands: Racialized trauma and the pathway to mending our hearts and bodies*. London: Penguin.

Mignolo, Walter D. 2009. 'Epistemic disobedience, independent thought and decolonial freedom', *Theory, Culture & Society* 26: 159–81.

Mills, China. 2018. 'Teaching white innocence in an anti-black racial order: British values and the psychic life of coloniality'. In *The Fire Now: Anti-racist scholarship in times of explicit racial violence*, edited by Azeezat Johnson, Remi Joseph-Salisbury and Beth Kamunge, 223–34. London: Bloomsbury.

Neufeld, Jonathan A. 2015. 'Aesthetic disobedience', *Journal of Aesthetics and Art Criticism* 73: 115–215.

Oliver, Adèle. 2023. *Deeping It: Colonialism, culture and criminalisation of UK Drill*. London: 404 Inklings.

Owusu, Melz. 2025. *Undisciplined: Reclaiming the right to imagine*. Hoboken, NJ: Polity.

Page, Cara and Erica Woodland. 2023. *Healing Justice Lineages: Dreaming at the crossroads of liberation, collective care, and safety*. Berkeley, CA: North Atlantic Books.

Palmer, Lisa Amanda. 2020. 'Diane Abbott, misogynoir and the politics of Black British feminism's anticolonial imperatives: "In Britain too, it's as if we don't exist"', *Sociological Review* 68(3): 508–23.

Phalafala, Uhuru Portia. 2020. 'Decolonizing world literature through orality'. In *Handbook of Anglophone World Literatures*, edited by Stefan Helgesson, Birgit Neumann and Gabriele Rippl, 193–208. Berlin: De Gruyter.

Richardson, Laurel. 1993. 'Poetics, dramatics, and transgressive validity: The case of the skipped line', *Sociological Quarterly* 34: 695–710.

Sandal-Wilson, Hakan and Natasha Tanna. 2020. 'The politics of writing in and with crises: A conversation with Dr Natasha Tanna' [blog post] *Methods in Question*. Accessed 19 July 2025. https://methodsinquestion.co.uk/blog/f/the-politics-of-writing-in-and-with-crisis.

Sirleaf, Matiangai. 2023. 'Rendering whiteness visible', *American Journal of International Law* 117: 484–7.

Snead, James A. 1981. 'On repetition in black culture', *Black American Literature Forum* 15(4): 146–54.

Spivak, Gayatri Chakravorty. 1988. 'Can the subaltern speak?', *Die Philosophin* 14: 42–58.

Stoever, Jennifer Lynn. 2016. *The Sonic Color Line: Race and the cultural politics of listening*. New York: New York University Press.

Taneja, Preti. 2022. *Aftermath*. New York: Simon and Schuster.

The Poet, George. 2024. *Track Record: Me, music, and the war on blackness*. London: Hodder & Stoughton.

Walker, Sharon. 2021. 'Whiteness and exclusion: An ethnography of the racialised discourse of the UK's Widening Participation agenda'. PhD thesis, University of Cambridge. https://doi.org/10.17863/CAM.64202.

Watkin, Christopher. 2022. *Biblical Critical Theory: How the Bible's unfolding story makes sense of modern life and culture*. Grand Rapids, MI: Zondervan Academic.

Weidler, Markus. 2020. 'Kristeva's thought specular: Aesthetic disobedience as a new form of revolt', *Southern Journal of Philosophy* 58: 456–84.

Zaino, Karen and Jordan Bell. 2022. 'We are each other's breath: Tracing interdependency through critical poetic inquiry', *International Studies in Sociology of Education* 31(1–2): 27–48.

Part II

Conversations for change: life stories of Black, queer and trans kinship and parenthood

3 Heather and Maggie

Haydn Kirnon

By some tacit agreement, my partner and I, of late, appear to have developed a penchant for watching films on a terrestrial TV channel that clearly caters for a very particular demographic. I can't quite bring myself to be more explicit – already, this feels like way too public an admission – except to say that almost all of the ads on this channel seem to feature walk-in bath tubs, incontinence pads, or a Nordic pleasure cruise on which a stylish, well-heeled, silver-haired, White heterosexual couple is seen gliding across, first, a sun-dappled ship deck, and then the same deck, but in moonlight, the glide having morphed into a snake-hipped, we've-still-got-it shimmy, to the accompaniment of a live band, before, finally, they are seen, glamorous, gleaming and gloating, seated at the captain's table for supper. It's strange, the two extremes of the third age presented in these ads: happening and hip or hip replacement; nothing in between. Occasionally, one of us will make a pithy observation about the recurring themes of these commercials, prompting the other to chuckle. As though, somehow, we've happened upon a phenomenon so alien, it couldn't possibly be targeted at us, but which, out of sheer perversity and fascination, we decide to continue watching. Regularly.

I am 58, my partner 64. What is unspoken between us is an awareness that we are not really fooling ourselves, but that we choose to perform doing so, because neither of us is quite ready to navigate just how much we are, in truth, implicated in the reality (or realities) that these commercials depict.

What we watch on this channel is almost always 'old' movies. Films from the 60s and 70s. Two decades that, give or take a year or six – the specific number of years between my partner and me – bookend our respective childhoods. His in the West Country, in an unbroken stretch, and mine, stretched between the Midlands and the Caribbean; not exactly broken but with several fault lines.

The films we watch are, mostly, B movies and British sex comedies, almost always entertainingly bad, but always streamed and filtered through the prism of our knowing, twenty-first-century ironic gaze. Our shared 'enjoyment' of these films represents a (pop-)cultural nexus; what I call the Venn diagrammatic overlap of my partner's childhood in the bosom of a White, working-class English family and mine, as the child of African-Caribbean parents, living first in a mining village in the Midlands, then in a village on the east coast of Barbados, before ending up once more in that same mining village in the Midlands. An 'expat' might say it was a … 'peripatetic' childhood; as the child of 'immigrants', though, 'sent back' to my mother's country of origin, I call it … 'fractured'.

The fare on offer, on this channel, serves our purpose as undemanding filmic comfort food, at the end of a long day. Occasionally, one of us might express amusement, or even shock, at the sexism, racism, misogyny or homophobia of what we're watching, but what I think we see, more than anything, and *feel*, and what keeps us watching, is a world that echoes what has, in our minds, become a rose-tinted movie version of our respective childhoods. A world in which, however difficult and challenging life actually was, we see things that take us back to homes in which we feel we enjoyed the comfort and safety that our parents had woven around us: furniture we sat on, food we ate, dresses and hairdos our mothers favoured, actors our fathers admired. A Dick-and-Dora, Bill-and-Ben, Terry-and-June, Dastardly-and-Muttley, Morecambe-and-Wise world order, in which Mum and Dad went to work on an egg; a Mars a day helped you work rest and play; faggots were … for 'dinner' (which, today, as middle-aged, first-generation middle-class men we would now call … 'lunch'); and in which we might have chanted, say, 'Eeny, meeny, miny, moe / Catch a nigger by his toe', playing out in the street, with our friends, before heading up the wooden hill to Bedfordshire of an evening. The sexism, racism, misogyny and homophobia with which these films are often, casually, shot through *could* take me to a dark place – one in which, for instance, my mum, newly arrived in 'the Mother Country', in the early 60s, is in Woolworths, 'Woollies', handing over her hard-earned cash for a pair of tights the colour of which is described as 'nigger brown' on the packaging – but glancing, anodyne observations apart, I gently push all that to one side and enjoy the carefully cosy unity of this occasional nostalgia-fest with my partner.

Because what we're watching is never so involved or absorbing that we can't let ourselves be distracted, from time to time, safe in the knowledge that it won't ruin our following of the usually slender plot or our entertainment, we'll often find ourselves scuttling down an internet rabbit hole, aided by our phones, in search of some useless bit of information about a film location, say, or a brand of brown sauce, or a nagging conviction that Villain No. 3 used to play a corporal in *It Ain't Half Hot Mum*. (I want, badly, to include what I feel is a missing vocative comma, between *Hot* and *Mum*, I need it to be known, but I can find no evidence that there has ever been one present in the official title of this programme. I am, however, shortly, to provide the reader with plenty of evidence to suggest that this is entirely a 'me' problem ...)

Recently, one such foray led me to the Wikipedia entry of an English stage and film actor. Born in 1901, he seems to have enjoyed a reasonably successful screen and stage career, without ever becoming an enduring household name. He appeared in films helmed by directors as well-known as Alexander Korda and Brian Forbes, went to the States, had some success on Broadway, but 'disliked Hollywood and did not stay long'. He was nominated for a Tony Award. Towards the end of his career and life, he played a number of character roles in film and on TV. He died in 1969. Already, I've forgotten exactly which film it was I saw him in and what it was about. I'd probably have forgotten him, too, by now, but for one, brief observation in the 'Personal Life' section of his Wikipedia entry: 'Decades after [his] death in 1969, it was suggested that he was homosexual ...'. A mere baker's dozen of words, but, somehow, they won't let me be, provoking, instead, dozens of complicated thoughts, feelings. These include:

Anger: this isn't what watching this channel is supposed to do for me. It's meant to make me feel like I'm seven again; like I'm eating Weetabix soaked in hot milk and topped with satisfyingly crunchy demerara sugar for breakfast, pretending that I'm Fanny Craddock, acting out the preparation of a complicated recipe for the (probably reluctant) audience that is my companion at the pale-yellow Formica table in my mother's kitchen, my little sister; camping it up before I knew what camp was, but going, curiously, unadmonished by either parent.

Yet *more* anger: '... it was suggested'? 'Homosexual'? Why does *that* passive construction, *this* verb, *that* noun feel like a slur? And a very dated one at that. What is this doing in an encyclopaedia entry, in the year 2024, couched in this way? To this day, when I read the word 'homosexual', in my mind, I hear the stress fall on the first syllable, and 'hom-' rhyming with 'vom-'; the way it always sounded in the strangled 1970s BBC RP[1] of newsreaders and TV presenters, in my childhood. Even then, the laboured 'I'm-pronouncing-it-this-way-because-I-studied-Greats-not-because-I-*am*-one' delivery struck me as distancing, disdainful, defensive.

Sadness: this man had a whole life, a long career in film and theatre, a Tony nomination; doubtless, he had desires, longings, loves, *love* ... And yet, over fifty years after his death, all of that is reduced to ... this? And by whom? Actually, not anger, now, but rage: roiling rage, on behalf of a man I did not know and had never heard of until this casual statement pricked the bubble of my comfort viewing.

Sadness again: he barely lived to see homosexuality decriminalised, *partially*, in 1967. He would have been 66. Two years older than my partner is now. I was born in 1966. How would he have felt? Happy that it had finally been decriminalised? *Partially*. Angry that it had come so late in his life? Sad? Rageful?

Anger, sadness and rage, now all rolled, roiling, into one: who has the right to do this? Where is the accountability? What about this man's dignity? Where is the light and shade, the complexity of his desires, his longings, his loves, his ... *love*?

Self-doubt: what *is* it about the use of the word 'homosexual' that troubles me in this context? Still.

By the time I was in my mid-teens, in the early eighties, I was firmly engaged in the losing battle that was the (reluctant) struggle to hide my sexuality. If my half-hearted attempts to perform heterosexuality were Dr Bruce Banner, my true queer self was the Incredible Hulk: a towering, raging, green queen, bursting to break free and laughing, defiantly, at my own unconvincing ridiculousness in affecting to be attracted to 'the opposite sex'. I say firmly engaged, affecting to be attracted ... In truth, this is only accurate, technically; is only so much semantics. I was actively chasing no skirt whatsoever (nor shirt, come to that), but I never *said* I was hom(rhymes-with-'vom')osexual, trusting, naively, that this would keep me under the radar, when all evidence was so glaringly (and often gleefully) to the contrary.

At this point, I was in Barbados, attending an all-boys grammar school at which a very specific type of heteronormative masculinity was modelled as the ideal: boys called each other by their surname; 'floggings' would be administered by the headmaster, triggered by in-class misdemeanours, the details of which would be entered into something known

[1] Received Pronunciation.

as ‘the Black Book’, for the head’s consultation. There was a cadet corps; male teachers were addressed as ‘Sir’, female teachers, ‘Ma’am’; any suggestion of homosexuality led to the suggested homosexuals in question being known, by their peers, forever more, by a girl’s name. To everyone around me, my behaviour suggested I was a homosexual, so, as a suggested homosexual, and because my first name began with H, and my peers lacked creativity and imagination, I came to be known as ‘Heather’, joining forces with the boy who would come to be my adored best friend and formidable ally, ‘Maggie’.

This was possibly the earliest instance I can recall of making a queer virtue out of the prevailing homophobic necessity. I didn’t relish being called Heather, but at least it meant that I stood out as one of the few boys that got to be known by a first name, and I found I rather liked the singularity and defiance of standing out. I still do. More importantly, though, it marked the beginning of my awareness, having had ‘Heather’ and homosexuality thrust upon me, correctly, in the case of the latter, that I had better stand up for myself, albeit in my own way, and make it clear to the other boys that I was as formidable a presence in their midst as any other boy, and that any attempt to intimidate me, physically or psychologically, would have consequences.

Effeminate. There it is. I’ve written it, which is like saying it out aloud, for an audience, for the first time. Surprisingly, not a little shocking, even after all this time. But also, and equally surprisingly, curiously, freeing. The *Oxford English Dictionary* describes the word thus: ‘ADJECTIVE *derogatory* (with reference to a man) having characteristics and ways of behaving traditionally associated with women and regarded as inappropriate for a man’. It’s strange. I don’t recall anyone ever actually using this word to refer to me, at least in my presence, and yet, when I was a teenager, this word, whenever I came across it, would seem to square up to me, accusing, from the printed page, like an actor breaking the fourth wall. Not only reductive and making incontrovertible something complex and intangible about me, but suggesting, arch and mealy-mouthed, that that thing was bad. Or, at least, ‘inappropriate’. For a … man. And I knew that I was meant to hate that thing in myself. And I sort of did. But mostly didn’t. Which made me angry, but also, perversely, defiant, wilful, cussed.

The path to who I am, now, on the cusp of my seventh decade, watching creatively and politically problematic B movies, interspersed with ads for stairlifts, was a tortuous and, occasionally, tortured one, until … well, it wasn’t. But eventually – and this is the important thing – it wasn’t. And it continues not to be. And I have Heather and Maggie to thank for that. Because Heather (like Maggie), it turned out, was what my daughter and some of the young women that I teach today might refer to as a 'bad b'; she 'clapped back'; 'gave zero fucks' and not a few kicks, when dragged into a fight. Once, in the first form, I remember a boy standing on the sidelines of a tussle in which I was involved, observing of my combat technique: 'Look at *her*! Kicking like Purdey!' Purdey was a character in the TV show *The New Avengers*; a spy and martial-arts expert, played by Joanna Lumley, whose signature body blow was a well-aimed karate kick that always came to land where it hurt, served with a sexy stiletto heel, which, in turn, was paired with a voluminously flared trouser or culotte (yes, I'm using the fashion singular: that's the girl/boy I was/am). I was both annoyed – 'I like being a boy!' – and thrilled – 'I *love* being Purdey!'.

Masters and mistresses – that's what we called them! – at the school would, generally, turn a blind eye to fighting among the boys, up to a point. I guess they thought it was … character-building; 'made a man of you' or whatever. I saw quite a bit of 'whatever', among the pupils at that school, some of it brutal, and, from the get-go, I was very clear that it was not for me. You sank or swam, and how you did it was up to you, but to survive, you had to *learn* to do it. So, for me, that meant, if being challenged to a fight, not backing down. The losing of the fight, I cottoned on quickly, wasn't the thing. The not being seen to back down was. I might have eschewed 'manly' fisticuffs in favour of elegant Purdey foot-flicks, but the pain and, more importantly, message delivered were identical to those meted out by the non-'effeminate' boys, the … 'manly' – is that the opposite of 'effeminate'? – boys.

But none of this could have been achieved alone. Throughout my time at that school, I had a constant companion whose friendship and loyalty were unswerving: 'Maggie'. This, of course, wasn't my friend's real name, but, his given name began with the letter M, so this and his ascribed effeminacy saddled him with 'Maggie', just as I had been landed with 'Heather'.

We entered that school at the age of eleven, among the brightest boys of our cohort, on the island, garnering top marks in the Common Entrance Exam, or Eleven Plus, as it was known. I don't recall the exact moment at which we met, but there is no memory that springs to mind in which Maggie isn't either by my side, or having my back, in all our time together at the school: we were inseparable. We had no politicised language to make sense of just how fundamentally different we were from our peers, but, clearly, we knew we were and were drawn to each other because of this.

Already, at eleven, Maggie was six feet tall and powerfully built. Somehow, he had persuaded his mother to buy him school shoes with a rather generous Cuban heel. Maggie, knowingly, parlayed the combination of his natural height and the added Cuban heelage into a trademark exaggerated, provocative teeter, as he slinked across the quadrangle, to and from classes, a fledgling supermodel before the word had been invented. He would tighten his thick, brown, leather belt – which it amused him to call a cummerbund, because this was what a particular type of very wide and brightly coloured belt, which was all the rage among the more stylish girls at his church, at the time, was known as – until it gave him a cinched-in waist and cartoon hips. His nails were long and carefully manicured. There was no official school regulation that any of these details flouted, and yet they clearly marked him out, it was decided by the 'manlies', as being someone who had to be known by a girl's name and must take all the flak that that entailed. But the joke, it turns out, was, mostly, on the people who chose to call him by a girl's name. Maggie was fearless and often outrageous. Sometimes, between classes, he would wander up and down the rows of desks in our classroom, pretending to be an air stewardess, holding aloft an imaginary tray, and affecting a bored, mid-Atlantic accent, drawling: 'Coffee, tea or me. Coffee, tea or me …', staring the 'manlies' in the eye, defiantly, all the while. Another favourite thing for him to do was walk closely behind some studiedly virile sixth-former, pretending to be in a desperate hurry, imploring, impatiently, 'Excuse me, miss. Excuse me, miss …', then, when the sixth-former spun around, irate, shrieking, '*Oh*. You're a *boy*!', before running off, screaming with laughter. And with me in tow, equally convulsed, always. Because I was Maggie's willing, egging sidekick. Happily. Always ready to join in the dare, but with Maggie always taking things that crucial one step farther than it was wise to go. Which, of course, made it just the right step – in our minds – to take. We got so good at running at breakneck speed, we'd have dominated track and field, if we could have been bothered. We couldn't: track and field were not, it was clear, to be bothered by the likes of us. Sometimes we'd get caught and pay the consequences, but it never didn't seem worth it, and I rejoice, now, in how unrepentant we were. We didn't think we were being subversive. We were just being us, and, somehow, the manlies never quite seemed to beat that out of us. Never came out on top.

I wasn't exactly what you would call an academic highflyer at that school. Little of what was on offer interested me. In biology, maths, chemistry, physics, history and all the tedious rest of it, I was a passenger. Anything to do with words, though, and how you might use them to craft stories, amuse, provoke, inform, titillate, cajole, seduce, even deceive … Well, that was my domain. English, of course. But also, modern languages, which, I now realise, years later, as a teacher of Spanish, provided me with a golden opportunity to peel off from everything challenging about who I really was, and the life I was really living, and give myself over to the necessary performativity involved in the learning of another language, and the way in which it invited you almost to play a character, take on a completely foreign identity, and to travel to somewhere far away from where and who you really were.

In the first form, we had a textbook, for French, that was called something like *Le Français en Direct*. Each chapter followed the adventures of a boy called Jean Leduc, in a series of rather pedestrian conversations with his friends. When called upon to read the words of Jean Leduc and his chums aloud, most of the boys in class would savage what *le pauvre Jean* and pals had to say, as they attempted to do just that: merely *read*. But not me. I'd get myself up in an imaginary beret and foulard and I would *become* Jean Leduc (or *l'un de ses amis*). This invited sniggers and derision on the part of many of the other boys, unsurprisingly, but my fascination with how I sounded as I did this, and the escapism of it, could not be dented. I would be in a world of my own, somewhere French and far away.

I loved a word for the way it sounded; sometimes even the way it looked. The mastery of words and their assembly into sentences and paragraphs, I soon learnt, often provided me with an out, where my physical combat skills didn't. Not only could I charm my language teachers with my way with words, it turned out that I could often sweet-talk my way out of trouble with my peers, too. Once, I commended a nemesis on the impressiveness of his 'halitosis', early in the day. Much later, walking across the quad, minding my own business, I suddenly felt an emphatic cuff on the back of my head: my nemesis, it seems, had finally got round to consulting a dictionary at some point in the intervening hours. Yes, it hurt, but I still recall, with pride, how much of an object of ridicule my nemesis became, for other boys in the class, as news of this particular display of my mastery of invective spread. Then there was the time that another boy in my year – let's call him 'Julie' (no one actually did, but I'm going to allow myself a little private joke, here) – a well-regarded athlete and the star of the local interschool athletics championships, decided that he was going to beat up anyone in the class who had not represented either their house or the school in any competitive enterprise. When it came to me, and as I screwed up my courage to 'Purdey' my way out of a hole, 'Julie' simply announced to the gallery: 'She's all right. She *spells*!', a reference to the fact that, for two years running, I had represented the school in the Barclays Interschool Spelling Bee – a big deal on the island, sponsored by Barclays Bank, and an exemplar of the pride with which the academic excellence of young Black boys and girls of my generation was viewed in the early, post-independence Barbados of my childhood, all heats being broadcast on national radio, the final on television. I had got through to the semi-finals in the first year, the finals in the second. Words had, literally, on this occasion, saved my hide.

Languages, then, were my domain and, in fact, the only one in which I either rivalled or outdid my friend Maggie, for Maggie was both a highflyer and an all-rounder, academically. He was brilliant at everything, and this, somehow, despite the ridicule for being Maggie, brought him very real, if grudging respect from many of the boys who would affect to despise us.

Maggie and Heather were inseparable. They would strut around, fearlessly, clutching piles of folders and books to their chest, hips swaying exaggeratedly, unrepentantly, like the Pink Ladies in *Grease*, oblivious to catcalls, as they ascended and descended flights of steps, between classes; arguing about who was cuter: Patrick Duffy as Bobby Ewing in *Dallas* (Maggie), or Greg Evigan as B. J., in *B. J. and the Bear* (Heather). Maggie would moon over one of our teachers, who taught biology, but also coached basketball, saying he had a 'Bobby body'. I didn't think that Greg Evigan resembled anyone in our immediate orbit, which is almost certainly why he was my preferred object of teenage lust.

For years, after leaving school, I kept memories of this friendship buried deep, even from myself. Choosing to see the shenanigans of Heather and Maggie as so much camp, superficial acting out. The reasons for this are complex and various, but, gradually, I came to realise that I was doing myself and Maggie a disservice.

There was a lot of complicated family 'stuff' going on for me, at home, outside of school, and it is only as an adult that I see glimpses of compassion and empathy in my friend's treatment of me that were beyond his years, as he quietly, discreetly, did what he could to assuage some of those difficulties. Coming from a more affluent background than I, he was always generous to a fault when it came to stumping up for extra tuck, to be shared; buying *Tiger Beat* and *Modern Screen* magazines that really didn't interest him, but which I longed to get my hands on, but could rarely afford, because the images of dreamy, 'dishy', non-threatening pretty-boy pin-ups, peddled in the former, and the old-school Hollywood glamour and tittle tattle, which were the stock in trade of the latter, fed my vivid imagination and the need for escape from an unsettled, unsettling home life. He was the only person to whom I ever spoke about the things that troubled me when I wasn't at school. He didn't offer counsel. He was only a child. We were only children. But he listened. He didn't judge. He kept my secrets.

Sometimes, we'd have petty rows. After running into me, outside of school, on three separate occasions in quick succession, the fact that – unfortunately, for me – I happened to be wearing exactly the same outfit each time – high-waisted, navy blue flares (I think we used to call them 'waisters'), with three big buttons on the wide waistband, and a tight-fitting white shirt, with navy blue buttons, blue stitching, and epaulettes; it was my version of something I'd seen Jaclyn Smith wear in an episode of *Charlie's Angels* and I loved it – led him to remark, publicly, and to much mirth, on the return to school, following the third sighting, that he had 'seen Kirnon in *the uniform* – AGAIN', which was the cause of a brief falling out. But these tiffs were always just that, a storm in a teacup, and we would make up promptly. I can't speak for him, but simply no one else around was as good a friend to me, and as much FUN. Because that's the thing. Our friendship wasn't one based solely on the need to be allies in a school that didn't encourage boys like us to *be* boys like us. It was one based on the need for support, yes, but also on loyalty, solidarity, dependability and sheer, unalloyed fun. It was based on each of us seeing ourselves in the other. On all of those things that the school should've been encouraging in everyone. Even boys like us. Only it didn't. So, we found our way to doing that for ourselves.

When I was 16, I left Barbados and went back to England, to continue my education. Maggie and I stayed in touch always but, inevitably, saw a lot less of each other. We would always hang out when I went back to the island to visit my grandmother, and he visited London once, memorably, in the late 90s. The friendship, though, had, by then, lost its adolescent momentum; our lives taking very different paths. The return to the UK began, for me, a long, but active and engaged journey towards realising a healthy queer identity for myself. Or at least my version of one. Maggie, though, didn't choose that path, and on that visit to London, the last time we would see each other, he expressed, not exactly dismay, but genuine bewilderment at my determination to take that path, to continue on it, and to insist on being openly queer. It was never censure or revulsion. Just genuine bafflement. Something beyond his ken. It just wasn't for him. Maggie died four years later.

Though Maggie did not, after we left school, choose either to be heterosexual or live as though he were, I am not at liberty to be more specific about the details of that life or even mention his real name.

A few years ago, when Facebook was in its infancy, a group was started for and by alumni of our year at school. Cautiously, I joined the group, never contributing, choosing, instead, to judge, silently, the predictable smugness and self-satisfaction evident in how these boys' lives had turned out: taught by the sons and daughters of the post-independence Bajan middle class, we'd been bred to take up 'the professions' and breed accordingly, in turn, and these boys hadn't disappointed, at least if their public-facing personas were any accurate indication. By their lights, a degree in Modern Languages and eking out a London living, as an openly hom(rhymes-with-'vom')osexual, journeyman translator in your late 30s did not spell success, and I kept schtum. Then, one day, a grainy, faded colour photograph was posted in the group, showing those of my peers who had gone on to sixth form at the school, after I had returned to the UK, back in the early 80s, ranged in rows on the steps of the assembly hall, staring confidently into the camera, arms crossed, legs spread, already rehearsing the self-assured hetero-swagger of the conservative lawyers, doctors, engineers and middle-to-high-ranking government functionaries that they would become. Everyone was tagged, many of them with whichever affectionate nickname they had picked up while at the school. My friend had been tagged simply 'Maggie'.

Even as I write this, I can still feel the rage and sadness I felt at that moment. Maggie had been the brightest boy in our year, leaving school with not only the highest grades of us all, but of all the sixth formers on the island, and going on to become a brilliant and well-respected doctor. Now he was gone and here was this mean, thoughtlessly-crafted little Facebook epitaph, reducing him to a name that had been dreamt up to humiliate and ridicule him. He didn't live to reclaim 'Maggie' the way that I have done 'Heather'; imbue her/him with queer agency and a sense of pride. I minded for him and for me. Just as I minded for that actor on whose Wikipedia page 'it was suggested that he was homosexual'. My friend had had a whole life – albeit one ended prematurely. He had had a successful career in medicine. He had had desires, longings, loves, *love* … and yet, years after his death, all of that was reduced to … this? And by whom? It is to my everlasting shame that, following much reflection, I chose not to deal with this matter directly, on the Facebook page, opting, instead, to withdraw from the group.

I've never asked myself where, in the early 90s, I got the courage to go on Pride marches; come to London, and find my gay, Black brethren; to help set up groups and workshops for the queer, Black men in my community; or, in the late 90s, become a Black, queer dad to a daughter with two Black queer mums. Because I've never thought of myself as courageous.

It is presumptuous of me to suppose that Maggie would have wanted to reclaim that identity from our school days together, publicly, himself, or for me to do so on his behalf; he might *not* have wanted me to take up the cudgels on Facebook, in his defence; however, it is undeniable that the seeds of the courage that I found to become that person, *this* person, were sown, all those years ago, by those two eleven-year-old boys/girls, and I celebrate and thank both of them, but especially Maggie, without whom those inspirational beginnings wouldn't have been possible, for their nerve, resilience, joy, laughter and solidarity. Thank you, girls/boys. Thank you, Heather and Maggie.

4
'If you're gay, you're lucky to be a parent': current issues for queer and trans families in the UK

Marcin W. Smietana

A person wrote in the chat box: 'thank you all so much for opening my mind to all the possibilities that are out there, I much appreciated all your stories'. Those thanks were addressed to the five people who spoke on the panel: all of them identified as LGBTQ+, all of them were parents or in the process of becoming parents through different kinds of reproductive pathways, and all of them became – often inadvertently – activists. The latter is so telling, if trying to have children as LGBTQ+ seems to invite one to become an activist: it means that it is still not a taken-for-granted life choice, not an obvious one, and not an easy one. In this chapter I therefore argue that having children as LGBTQ+ often requires some kind of engagement with activism for reproductive rights and justice. The stories of the five activists and parents give rise to this chapter. It is based on the creative methods event, Current Issues for Queer and Trans Families: Activist Roundtable, that took place online in November 2021 within the research network 'Global conversations towards queer social justice' I co-convened with Natasha Tanna and Hakan Sandal-Wilson at the University of Cambridge. In that session in November we had conversations with five LGBTQ+ parent-activists who have all been doing prominent work for LGBTQ+ families across the UK: Jackie Fernandez (New Family Social), Freddy McConnell (Equality for Trans Families), Richard (writer and speaker), Erika Tranfield (founder of Pride Angel) and Alan White (director of Surrogacy UK). In 2021, all five activists gave their consent to the publication of the recording from the event and, in 2025, all of them were also able to approve and update the current written version. In this chapter, I do my best to retell their five reproductive stories, as they speak for themselves. These are stories of how LGBTQ+ family projects may become thinkable (Pralat 2018;

Smietana 2019) and feasible, even though 'if you're gay, you're lucky to be a parent', as one of the speakers, Alan, said (Current Issues for Queer and Trans Families 2021).

The event this chapter builds on (held in 2021), and the writing of this chapter three years later (in 2024 and 2025), refer to the UK context, where LGBTQ+ activists have been fighting for full social and political recognition, including reproductive rights and justice. Thanks to this, many LGBTQ+ family rights have been gradually recognised in the UK, including the rights to adopt children, in 2005, to carry out surrogacy, in 2010, and to enter same-sex marriages, in 2014 in England, Wales and Scotland, and in 2020 in Northern Ireland. However, these rights – as well as the social awareness and support for them – are still relatively new. And as the stories in this chapter demonstrate, heteronormativity is still rampant and pervasive. Only three and a half decades ago, in 1988, Margaret Thatcher's government introduced the infamous Section 28 of the Local Government Act, banning any description of gay and lesbian relationships as 'pretended family relationships' and prohibiting teaching about homosexuality at school. Section 28 was revoked only two and a half decades ago, in 2000 (Weeks 2017). Despite the social and legal advancements, creating queer kinships and families, in particular families with children, is still not an obvious or an easy matter for LGBTQ+ identified people in the UK (Pralat 2018; Schorscher-Pecu 2021; Department of Health and Social Care 2023). For this reason, LGBTQ+ families continue to organise for social and reproductive justice today. Socio-economic status, social awareness, and the heteronormativity of the law and public healthcare continue to impact LGBTQ+ access to reproductive options (Smietana 2025). In this context, we invited LGBTQ+ family activists to speak about their reproductive life stories, and their engagement with activism.

Creative critical interventions

In terms of research methods, this chapter argues that conventional forms of social science research could benefit from incorporating more horizontal participation and voices of people from marginalised communities – being mindful, however, of not burdening them with the 'minority tax' of having to undertake social-justice work. Indeed, centring individual and community voices has been long pioneered by ethnographic, qualitative and other researchers telling the stories of their research participants in ways that foregrounded individual and community cases. However, only some of them grounded their storytelling approaches in a clear commitment to social justice (Twine 2010; Golombok 2015; Cromer et al. 2024), and only recently has the growing prominence of research impact in research evaluations given rise to more horizontal approaches that may challenge the hierarchies of knowledge production. The latter have long been criticised by activist movements such as Reproductive Justice, which stemmed from community activism of women of colour in the United States and gradually made its way into academia (Sistersong 2007; Ross and Solinger 2017). These contributions inspired us for collaborative work with Charis Thompson and France Winddance Twine, as we invited scholars of reproductive justice and those of queer reproduction to think together at the 'Making Families' symposium at UC Berkeley (Smietana et al. 2018, 123). Collaborative initiatives bridging academia and society have also been developed in areas such as LGBTQ+ life stories, for example where life story diaries were written by Polish LGBTQ+ people in response to a call by an academic research team (Bednarek et al. 2022).

The transformative potential of linking together both life storytelling and a commitment to social justice was crystallised by the academic, activist and artistic project and series of online events, Creaction: Creative Critical Interventions for Social Justice, run by the editors of this volume in 2021 (Creaction 2021). Some of the underlying ideas – such as the politics of writing (Sandal-Wilson and Tanna 2020) were also developed by two of the editors, earlier within the seminar series, Methods in Question: Epistemologies of Gender and Sexuality, at the University of Cambridge (Methods in Question 2018). And this eventually led to another collaborative research network, Global Conversations Towards Queer Social Justice (2021), convened by Hakan Sandal-Wilson, Natasha Tanna and myself at the University of Cambridge in 2021–2. Through a series of online biweekly events, we aimed to build conversations between scholars, activists and artists, with a commitment to fostering social justice through creative forms of expression as well as centring marginalised individual and community stories.

One of those online events gave rise to this chapter. It featured reproductive life stories presented by five LGBTQ+ parents and activists from across the United Kingdom, followed by a discussion, and attended by several dozen participants from across the globe. The following sections of the chapter present an edited version of these five reproductive life stories, followed by concluding remarks. All the five speakers expressed their written consent to sharing their stories publicly online and under their real names, and the event recording is available online

(Current Issues for Queer and Trans Families 2021). In 2025, the chapter draft was also read and updated by all the participants, following which I addressed their feedback.

All of the five speakers identified as LGBTQ+: two of them as lesbian, two as gay and one as transgender. All of them pursued some form of activism for the sake of families with LGBTQ+ parents. Four of them had children at the time of the event and one was an intended parent who had a child soon after the event. The means they used to create families included adoption, donor conception (both in fertility clinics and through home insemination), as well as surrogacy in the UK and overseas. One of the speakers was single and four had partners. However, there was no speaker who would have represented coparenting or multi-parent family models. Three of the speakers were White British, one identified as British Asian and one as Black British Caribbean.

The chapter also contextualises these five accounts against the broader background of a qualitative interview research study I carried out, between 2020 and 2023, with 30 families created through surrogacy by gay men living in the UK. Of the 30 families, 28 were couples and two consisted of single people. The men, aged twenty-four to fifty-two, were in the process of surrogacy or had young children. They were UK residents with 22 different national identifications. Twenty-three families identified as White, and seven were multi-ethnic couples, where one partner identified as: Latin American / Filipino / South Asian / British South Asian / Black British Caribbean / Ghanaian / British Nigerian. The study received clearance from the Sociology Ethics and Risk Assessment for Research (SERAR) process at the University of Cambridge.

By 'reproductive life stories' I mean the stories told by people about their reproductive lives – that is, stories they tell about what they understand as reproduction in their own lives. In conceptualising the term, I draw on Faye Ginsburg's (1989) work on 'procreation stories': women's 'narratives ... so frequently concerned with transitional reproductive events as well as women's relationship to both biological and social reproduction' (13). In their life stories, grassroots abortion activists that Ginsburg spoke to in an American community were 'consciously connecting their own experience – biographical and historical – to their commitment to the abortion issue'. Thus, their life stories became their procreation stories, as transitional reproductive events revealed 'the dissonance they felt between the conditions they faced – for example, becoming a mother – and the available cultural resources for structuring that change, cognitively and socially'. Likewise, the parent-activists whose stories are featured in this chapter consciously connected their reproductive life stories to their activism. These stories follow in the sections below.

At the roundtable event that inspired this chapter, we first asked the five speakers: 'We'd like to hear your family stories, to the extent that you can share them. How did you get to have a family?' Second, we also asked them what they thought the current issues were for LGBTQ+ people's families – or, translating this question to a more personal level, why and how they had become involved in different forms of activism or public activity for the community.

Freddy

> It's interesting listening to your introduction, Marcin, about the sort of three questions you posed about how we became family, what are the issues currently facing parents like us, and then sort of what our activism looks like. I don't honestly think I could separate those three things in my own personal situation. They are kind of the same question, I feel.

These words by Freddy McConnell – a writer, journalist and trans solo dad by choice, and the protagonist of the film *Seahorse* (2019) – made me realise what also transpired from the testimonies of the other LGBTQ+ parents taking part in the same event (Current Issues for Queer and Trans Families 2021): that becoming an LGBTQ+ parent may amount to becoming an activist – whether it is formal activism within civil society organisations and charities, or informal everyday activism within the communities one lives in. In other words, by the very attempt to become parents, LGBTQ+ people inadvertently place themselves in a position where they may need to fight against dominant social norms in order to make their path to parenthood possible and liveable.

Freddy divided the issues facing trans parents in the UK into two categories: the first one being medical, in terms of accessing the National Health Service (NHS) and what happens after that, and the other barrier being legal issues they face. He said he did not think there could be a trans parent in the UK who was not affected by those issues, because, in his experience 'we're still sort of in the dark ages when it comes to recognising trans parents in all sorts of ways'.

Freddy gave birth to his son in 2018, as a trans dad. He carried a pregnancy created through donor conception with donor sperm. However, in order to make it happen, he had to go through a change in his consciousness: 'I had to unlearn a lot of the stuff that I'd been taught. And then on top of that, I had to unlearn a lot of the sort of fear and shame I felt around the desire to become a parent'. He came out as a transgender man when he was finishing up university, in his mid twenties. When he first started transitioning in 2012, in the gender clinic he attended in London, he was told that testosterone would make him sterile. He recalls:

> And part of the process was getting to the gender clinic in London I was being referred to. And part of the conversation that we started having very early on was around testosterone and transition, medical transition. That was the assumption. It was also what I wanted.
>
> But even back then, this would have been 2011, 2012, things were much more rigid than I understand they are today. So you go to the gender clinic and you enter this one medical pathway of – and they use language like – becoming a man or becoming a woman.
>
> And even though that's not how most trans people actually understand our experiences.
>
> And with that came a discussion of infertility or sort of a brief mention of it.

Given the gender clinic's narrative of gender transition as a transition to infertility, Freddy thought he could always try to adopt a child in the future, because he had always wanted kids, he had always wanted to be a parent, and he never really imagined how it would happen. Yet about two years later, he came across a video on YouTube of a pregnant trans man. If it had not been for that, he says, he might not have become a parent, he might not know that was possible for him. 'So we're misinformed by our doctors on the NHS, it's just standard', he concludes, adding that it is now only exacerbated by the anti-trans media environment in the UK. Whereas 'the reality is we actually know there is emerging evidence that testosterone does not cause infertility; trans men and non-binary people can conceive … no matter how long they have been on testosterone'. This misinformation, according to Freddy, may at least partly be based on the fact that oestrogen does cause infertility in trans women and nonbinary people who were assigned male at birth.

Thus, Freddy stopped testosterone, conceived, had a healthy pregnancy and had the birth he wanted. Then he restarted testosterone and quite quickly got back to where he was in terms of his personal comfort and medical transition. He says:

> I think there's a misconception that people think trans men will find pregnancy itself very traumatising, very hard, but actually it's not. It's the kind of structural barriers that we face that are much more of a difficulty. And the assumptions, the assumptions that we're going to find it hard can be difficult to overcome.

The medical issue ended at this point for Freddy. However, as soon as his child was born, he faced another set of challenges, which were legal. There is just no legal recognition for trans men/masc people (trans men, assigned female at birth who identify as men, or people who present or identify in a masculine way regardless of assigned sex or specific gender label) who give birth in the UK, neither in the Births and Deaths Registration Act 1953, nor in the Human Fertilisation and Embryology Acts of 1990 and 2008, nor other laws. Even the Gender Recognition Act 2004 does not consider this possibility, 'because back then there was no imagining that trans people would one day become parents post transition', as Freddy points out. The Gender Recognition Act was meant to grant recognition for trans people who become parents post-transition: if, for example, a trans man is married to a cis woman and she carries their baby (via donor sperm), then he is the father. Vice versa, it also works for trans women, who can register as second female parent. It also says that those who are already parents when they transition retain the rights and responsibilities according to their sex assigned at birth. Yet a trans man/masc person who gives birth must be registered as a 'mother' even if they have transitioned to male. As Freddy explains:

> I think it is important to distinguish here between trans men/masc people who give birth and trans people who become parents without giving birth (be they women, men or nonbinary) … What was and is lacking – what wasn't imagined – was that a trans man/masc would retain the ability to get pregnant and give birth post-GRC [Gender Recognition Certificate], not because sterility is a legal requirement but because it was literally just not thought a rational possibility.

Thus, Freddy filed a court case to try and be registered as the father or the parent on his child's birth certificate:

> And the judge dealt with this by deciding that 'mother' is no longer a gendered term because women and transgender men can be

mothers. And it doesn't invalidate my gender recognition certificate, doesn't make me legally not a man any more, I'm just a man for some purposes, and then a woman or a mother for parenthood. The judgement does say (or must be interpreted as saying) I am both a man and a woman according to different laws. This is because some family laws, i.e. laws pertaining to parenthood, talk about 'women' not 'mothers'. Hence the judgement is legally incoherent (my opinion of course but far from only mine).

As a result, at the time of the event when we spoke (in 2021), Freddy said he felt 'left in a limbo state': his child did not have a birth certificate because his court case was ongoing. At that time, he was also pregnant with his second child, and he was considering giving birth in Sweden, given the UK legislation did not recognise him as a father.

The process of achieving 'procreative consciousness' (Berkowitz 2007; Smietana 2019) that Freddy talked about is common for LGBTQ+ people who become parents. LGBTQ+ people, historically, have been excluded from reproduction – and from the social power it endowed. This continues to happen today in many jurisdictions, such as Poland or Italy (Smietana 2024). Thus, research shows that LGBTQ+ people often go through a process of gaining queer reproductive consciousness, so that their self-awareness of identifying as LGBTQ+ will not exclude or contradict their self-awareness of being capable of creating or parenting human life.

Such a process often requires standing up against dominant social and legal norms, and thus, becoming an activist in some way, as Freddy said at the beginning of his reproductive story. Freddy and other trans fathers have managed to become parents. However, what is yet to be dismantled are the medical assumptions that testosterone therapy precludes pregnancy, as well as legal barriers for birthing trans men and nonbinary people to be recognised as fathers or even simply as parents.

Jackie

Like Freddy, the lesbian couple Jackie Fernandez and her partner Tor also sought their way to becoming parents, without much community support or a clear road map. And like Freddy, they managed to overcome social norms that put them at a disadvantage, as intended parents. As a result, both Freddy and Jackie with Tor became activists over time. Freddy became a campaigner for trans parenting rights and a film protagonist. And Jackie and Tor became activists for LGBTQ+ adoption rights within a major national charity.

In England, the statistics say that one in five adoptions are by same-sex couples – which does not include LGBT single adopters and foster carers (New Family Social 2023). Jackie and her partner Tor are one of those same-sex couples: they adopted their son twelve years ago, when he was 13 months old. They are also parents to two children they conceived in a fertility clinic: a daughter, aged 16, and a son, aged 19 at the time of writing.

In 1999, Jackie met her partner, Tor Doherty, and by 2004, they started talking about having children – which was very difficult back then. They discovered that out of all fertility clinics in England, at the time, there were only two that would accept same-sex couples. However, as soon as they got there, they encountered financial barriers due to the heteronormativity that exists in the structure of fertility treatment. These barriers persist today in the UK, despite an announcement by the Sunak government that this was going to be changed (Schorscher-Pecu 2021; Department of Health and Social Care 2023). Jackie recalls:

> So it was very interesting when we went there. Basically, there were two prices: for heterosexual couples because they could get IVF treatment for free; but for same-sex couples we had to pay the full whack. And that was a lot of money each month if you wanted to have a child.

Jackie got pregnant first, but after 'quite a long, long, arduous task', she then had a miscarriage. Therefore, she swapped with her partner, Tor, who became pregnant with their eldest son, born in 2006. Their daughter was born in 2009. Back then, there was no legal relationship in terms of recognising Jackie as the children's other parent, so she had to apply to adopt them – thus, her children, who were conceived by her partner, now have adoption certificates rather than their own birth certificates. Jackie had to go through an adoption process because until recently there was no formal way that partners of same-sex couples could be on birth certificates.

In 2011, Jackie and Tor decided to pursue adoption. 'There was more space in our family', Jackie reminisced, 'and we always had adoption in mind'. Once again, they struggled to find an agency:

> because, as you can see, we're a mixed-heritage couple, and our children are mixed-heritage. And where I live in Cambridgeshire,

> the social worker was really honest. She said, 'look, we haven't got any mixed-heritage children in Cambridge' [at the time in 2011]. So we went on what is called a national register.

The couple's attempt to match their skin colour to their children's confirms a pattern found by research on families created by lesbian, gay and heterosexual parents through reproductive technologies. Intended parents seek racialised resemblance with their children not only to emphasise a sense of belonging within the family they aim to create, but also to fend off potential stigmatisation multi-ethnic and interracial families often face in a society that continues to naturalise resemblance as a proxy for kinship (Smietana and Twine 2022).

Jackie and Tor had to go through an adoption agency. They found it hard to find an agency that would accept same-sex couples, but they eventually succeeded. They were very proactive about looking for children, as Jackie notes. On a cold January day, they went to an adoption event at Walsall stadium. They picked up 'loads of paperwork about these children' and they went through the files, over a coffee. And among them, they found their son. From the social worker who was looking after the boy, the couple received a report about him. As Jackie shares: 'And by then, our hearts were melted, and we went through the adoption process with him ... And he's just the light of our life, and he fits in just beautifully into our family'.

Jackie observes that 'a lot of the children ... have had losses in their first year of being born in this planet: they've lost their birth parents, they could have lost their foster carers'. Indeed, Jackie and Tor's son did. However, she encourages intended parents not to get scared:

> You'll have to support them with that for the rest of their lives. But you shouldn't write yourself off ... if you think you've had a mental health problem. That's actually a really good thing if you're showing that you've actually sought support. And you actually learn from it. And you're better for it. It's a positive thing.

For over a decade now, Jackie and her partner Tor have been volunteers and board members for New Family Social – a national organisation that has been supporting LGBTQ+ adopters and foster carers since 2007. With over 5,500 members today, the organisation runs training for social workers, in LGBTQ+ awareness, trans awareness and gender diversity. Moreover, Jackie is also an independent member, vice chair and chair of several adoption and fostering panels, which make recommendations about whether people are suitable to adopt and whether it is the right match for the child.

Some of the barriers that Jackie and Tor faced on their path to parenthood have been removed in the UK today: fertility clinics and adoption agencies are open to LGBTQ+ intended parents, and same-sex partners can appear together on children's birth certificates. However, within NHS healthcare, gamete donation and IVF continue to be provided on the grounds of a medical definition of infertility, which may not apply to LGBTQ+ intended parents. The previous government's announcement that this is bound to change (Department of Health and Social Care 2023) is yet to be applied.

Erika

Erika Tranfield is the director and founder of Pride Angel, an organisation that helps connect people who want to become parents, coparents or donors. She is also a mum to three girls. Similarly to the other parent-activists characterised in this chapter, she also became an activist out of necessity. She says that she had always known she wanted to be a parent. Erika desired to find a sperm donor whom she could meet face-to-face and 'know who he was', as she explains, alongside the ability to keep in contact 'for the children to be able to know where they came from'. She says:

> It was quite important to actually find somebody who was going to be in our life, but that I actually understood who they were in order to be able to know whether it was right or wrong ... and I wanted for the donor to actually choose us also ... I also believe strongly that the donor should have a choice in choosing the recipient too.

Yet when Erika began searching for the donor in 2009, she realised that the limited information fertility clinics provided about known donors would not enable her to find who she was looking for. She was able to search for donors on basic criteria, such as eye colour and hair colour, but she did not get a lot of information about the personality and the individual. As an alternative to the clinic route, she also looked on the internet, but what she found 'there was a lot of men that were offering sex', which, as a lesbian, was not a route she wished to take. Erika recalls:

> And the fertility clinic route was again, something that I wasn't too fond on using a donor from, because I didn't have the ability to meet the donor ... So at that moment in time, because there was no service available to help find a known donor, I decided to set up Pride Angel. So Pride Angel was set up with the intent to help find a sperm donor, a known sperm donor, but also to help fill that gap ...

Following the creation of Pride Angel, Erika tried four different sperm donors, using home insemination. On the last attempt, she conceived. Erika used the same donor for all three daughters she conceived with her wife Kelly, who also carried their third child using the same sperm donor. Even though Erika had her second child together with her wife Kelly, it is only Erika who is on the birth certificate, as the birth mother is always registered as such and they were not married or in a civil partnership at the time. For their third daughter, as they are now married, they are both on the birth certificate, but, as Erika notes, this is very unjust for their family. Both partners are automatically legal parents only when the conception occurs through donor insemination, if married or in a civil partnership, or through fertility treatment at a licensed UK clinic, and not through home insemination. By contrast, as Erika observes, a heterosexual couple can conceive at home without being married and both be on the birth certificate. The fact that same-sex couples cannot both be registered on the birth certificate in the case of home insemination – as heterosexual couples can – is something that Erika would like to address.

Like the other parent-activists whose accounts are discussed in this chapter, Erika also embarked on her activist project out of necessity. She set up Pride Angel to create a platform for potential parents, coparents and donors to meet without the need to use fertility clinics and their donor catalogues. This project has been successful, as Pride Angel is one of the major family creation organisations in the UK today, and not only for LGBTQ+ parents.

Richard

Richard is a writer, speaker, marketing professional and parent via gestational surrogacy in the United States. He lives in London with his husband and their two young children. Before venturing on the path to parenthood, Richard contacted other families of gay fathers and attended events for LGBTQ+ families, in order to understand the options he and his husband had, to become parents. They also had to actively work against the barriers imposed by the social organisation of sexuality and biology. As Richard recalls:

> So my husband and I have pretty much always talked about being parents. And it's something that we talked about very early in our dating days, because I think, for both of us, it was a bit of a deal breaker if the other person didn't feel the same … At the time, we didn't really understand or know how it would happen, because we weren't really sure about the options available to us. But one thing that we both agreed on, that we didn't want our sexuality or biology to prevent us from taking this journey and achieving our dream of parenthood. So when the time was right, we attended a lot of seminars, we did a lot of research, and we spoke to the very few people that we knew who'd done it before, just to try and understand the various routes to parenthood.

They opted for surrogacy because they wanted to have distinct biological links to their children. They settled on the US because they felt that that was where the legal framework was best, and that seemed to be the most secure option for them. When undertaking their first surrogacy arrangement, they also wanted to move quickly, which, at a cost, they could do in the US. 'The process itself was quite procedural, for want of a better phrase', Richard explains. On making the connections with the clinics and agencies in the state of Idaho, the couple had to fill in multiple forms. They were matched to the potential surrogate and the egg donor. Like Jackie and her partner in the previous testimony, Richard and his husband are also a mixed-race couple: Richard identifies as Black and his partner as White. Therefore, they sought a mixed-race egg donor to reflect their own multi-ethnic family composition and thus enhance the sense of belonging the children could potentially feel, as well as to give an impression of a coherent family unit (Smietana and Twine 2022). This was followed by 'a lot of paperwork'. Luckily, after a successful first transfer, their son was born. Yet upon the return to the UK, the couple needed another six months' worth of paperwork: they applied for a parental order, to get Richard and his husband recognised in the UK as their son's parents, which was eventually granted to them in February 2019. In a broader research study I conducted with 30 families of gay men, created through surrogacy in the UK or overseas, I characterised this process as 'spreadsheet fertility' (Smietana 2025) to capture the complexity of the fertility journey for gay men using surrogates and also for the complex labour of fertility planning and deliberation this involved.

Like the other LGBTQ+ parents in this chapter, Richard says that becoming an activist was not something he ever set out to do:

> It's just that the more I talk about this, and I do kind of talk about our journey and surrogacy issues at quite a few events and things like that, and the more I do that, the more I realise that there are some significant societal issues, I guess, and legal issues that can be sticking points for queer parents or intended parents pursuing an alternative route … Things are very much far from level, to put it bluntly, and it's really complicated or it can be really complicated for people in the position that I was in three years ago or four years ago. And even beyond birth, in those early years of parenthood, there are issues that just continue through.

Based on his experience, Richard categorises the relevant issues into three areas: workplace, life with the toddler, and legislation. Regarding the workplace, when his son was born, Richard took almost a year off to look after him. As he says, he was lucky enough to work for an employer who supported this and wanted to champion LGBTQ+ inclusion policies. Thanks to the legal basis that exists in the UK, as a parent through surrogacy, Richard was able to obtain adoption leave, which is equal to maternity leave. However, having friends who are in a similar position to his has shown Richard that not everyone's employer is that supportive. Gender stereotyping and an unconscious bias in many workplaces make it difficult to request parental leave or even childcare leave or emergency visits to nursery or to pick up one's child. He says:

> I've heard instances where, you know, dads, not necessarily gay dads, have been denied that opportunity to go and pick up their child if they need to, because the assumption is that there's a mother there that would do that, and that is her role to do that … And my family dynamic meant that our workplace had to do a lot of learning. It was a steep learning curve for them, but thankfully it wasn't too much of an issue. And I, in many ways, became kind of the poster boy for how to do it, because they wanted to be this inclusive company, but they'd never had that case in point until I came along and requested all of these things, which were not, you know, unreasonable. It's just what a straight person would get or a mother would get. So it was just trying to balance that out.

As Richard felt he needed to teach his employer how to approach gay dad families, he gradually undertook a kind of everyday activism in his workplace. In his account, he also links conversations in the workplace to an awareness of LGBTQ+ families in broader society. Thus, he thinks that 'the more that we have events like this [Current Issues for Queer and Trans Families 2021] and the more that, you know, the new cycle continues the way that it is, hopefully it will become more acceptable and easier to have those conversations in the workplace'.

Second, as a gay father and a male primary caregiver of a toddler, Richard has been facing fairly rigid gender norms. Advertising and socialising for many activities and groups a parent might join with their baby are 'heavily geared to mums on maternity leave'. He says: 'And that was quite difficult for us or for me as the primary caregiver to find a safe space where I could assimilate into and make friends and have play dates and things like that'. According to him, the traditional family structure is so ingrained that it can make a gay dad either an outsider or a novelty. He shares: 'And so, for example, when I walk into mum and baby yoga, the first, you know, the first question is, what are you doing here? Or are you babysitting? Or is it dad's day to have the baby?'. Hence his activist approach in his daily life:

> So there are a lot of things there that it's not easy to change because a lot of it is cultural. But again, the more that, you know, the more visibility that we have in terms of our alternative family structures, the more we can hopefully see a change with that … I've spoken to a lot of the organisers and just pointed out the way that can make non-mums feel when they walk into that … So essentially, we need to get to a place where alternative parenting journeys are normalised so that we're no longer different and invite questions at mum and baby yoga.

Lastly, Richard mentions the legal side. In his view, the UK surrogacy laws are outdated and in need of change. Indeed, the UK surrogacy community has also been campaigning for surrogacy law reform (Law Commission 2023). The outdated character of the current UK surrogacy laws, according to Richard, often makes people like him go abroad and spend huge sums of money on surrogacy. What is more, without the right guidance, they can go to risky markets, where bringing their child home or even just being recognised as parents is not straightforward. Eventually, even upon return to the UK, parents through surrogacy 'face a mountain of paperwork, even just to be named as parents'. Indeed, in the surrogacy study I carried out among 30 families of gay dads in the UK, between 2020 and 2023, eight families travelled to the US or Canada for surrogacy. Among the reasons for reproductive travel overseas, they mentioned their HIV+ status, relatively long waiting times in the UK, social and cultural skills required for networking within the UK surrogacy community, and risks linked to the fact that, in surrogacy in the UK, parental orders for intended parents are granted only after the child's birth (Law Commission 2023).

Alongside these barriers, of great relevance are also the financial challenges that many LGBTQ+ intended parents face. In my study of surrogacy arrangements undertaken by gay men living in the UK (Smietana 2025), I found that all of the 30 families I interviewed had annual household incomes above the UK average, and none of them received any funding from the NHS (for IVF, for example), contrary to heterosexual couples that do receive (albeit to a varied extent) NHS-funded fertility treatments.

In sum, Richard's activism originated inadvertently, as he contacted some gay fathers he knew and as he attended events and seminars for LGBTQ+ families, in order to understand how he could become a parent together with his husband. When he did become a parent and a primary caregiver for his and his husband's son, Richard also realised he needed to undertake everyday activism in his workplace, as well as within mum and baby groups he attended, given he was often the first or the only gay dad in the company or group. This led him to think that if there was more social awareness of LGBTQ+ families, the personal conversations that he and other parents in similar positions have at work and in daily life would also be easier. Thus, he became a public speaker and an activist for gay family rights.

Alan

At the moment when the event this chapter draws on took place (Current Issues for Queer and Trans Families 2021), Alan White was an intended parent through traditional surrogacy, together with his husband. Around a year later, the couple's son was born. Alan is also the director of Surrogacy UK (SUK), one of the largest non-profit surrogacy organisations in the UK. SUK promotes a particular model for altruistic surrogacy, which is based on friendship between surrogates and intended parents.

Alan's personal story is also linked to his activism. Similarly to Freddy, whose account is above, Alan went through a process of gaining 'procreative consciousness' as a gay person. He was born in an industrial town in Cumbria in 1980, and he came out when he was 22 and studying at university in Manchester. At that point, he thought that being gay was not compatible with having children. He shares:

> I'm saying that because I think that one of the challenges I've had personally is that when I came out, I kind of gave up the idea of being a parent for a time. Being a family, being a parent had always been kind of part of my story, I guess, or part of what I envisaged my future to be. But it was something that I lost when I came out. And perhaps now I know that I didn't need to lose that. But I think in terms of things that I'm passionate about, it's encouraging young gay and trans people these days, that there are these alternative routes to parenthood, that you don't need to give up on that.

In contrast, Alan's husband, whom he met 15 years ago, had a different kind of experience. Alan explains:

> He'd never had a coming out moment, but had always known and had never had that thing of giving up on becoming a parent. So he was very clear that if we were going to be together, we were going to have kids. And I kind of said, I need some time to think about it. Because when you've unlearned or kind of written kids out of your future, out of your story, it does take some time, I think, to bring them back in. So I said, give me five years. And five years later, we began to think about how we would become parents.

The couple considered all of the options, and eventually decided on surrogacy. Initially, Alan found the thought of surrogacy very difficult and he was much more in favour of adoption. This was because, as he says, 'I saw a process in adoption, which I understood. And I saw an end point at which there would be a decision'. Apparently, this seemed very different in surrogacy. Yet 'there is more structure if you know where to go', notes Alan. Similarly to Richard, the gay dad through international surrogacy whose story I discussed above, and like all men in the 30 surrogacy families I interviewed in the UK between 2020 and 2023, Alan resorted to surrogacy organisations: 'if you go to particular organisations and things, there is that kind of structured pathway to parenthood, and we decided on Surrogacy UK from several organisations that we looked at, they felt like the best match for us'.

Within SUK, Alan and his husband met Emma, who became a 'traditional surrogate', that is one using her own ova without the help of an egg donor. They tried to conceive through home inseminations for two years, which involved three miscarriages, until they finally succeeded with a pregnancy that resulted in the birth of their son.

Around the time that he met Emma, Alan got involved as a director of Surrogacy UK, as he says, 'kind of because I wanted to give something back to make sure that this organisation still exists in the future', even if he has never considered himself an activist. One of the things he is passionate about is 'general awareness and celebration of alternative routes to parenthood'. He links this passion to his own past experiences:

> Thinking back to me as a kid, would my coming out, would my kind of story of my sexuality really have been different if I was more aware of things? I imagine that's still a very current issue. And particularly I think for young people who are questioning their sexuality, but are in families where family is really important, you know, and where that's all, you know, one of the key goals of their future is to become a father or a mother. And what impact that recognition of sexuality has on those people at that time in their life, which is really difficult. And I think, you know, celebrating and making people aware of gay parenthood and these routes to it is really important.

This kind of social awareness would also mean greater equality. And it is campaigning against different kinds of inequalities that Alan is particularly passionate about. A closely related issue he mentions is affordability of surrogacy, given it is often very expensive. For this reason, Alan promotes models such as at SUK, where accessibility and inclusivity feature in the organisation's goals. In the UK, altruistic surrogacy is legal, whereby the surrogate is compensated for the necessary expenses but she offers her reproductive labour on an altruistic basis. This also increases the accessibility of surrogacy in the UK. However, even altruistic surrogacy has a cost. Among the 30 families I spoke to in the UK surrogacy study (Smietana 2025), the lowest cost of a traditional surrogacy arrangement was almost £13,000, which included the compensation of necessary expenses to the surrogate, cross-country travels to SUK meetings and for home inseminations, as well as some additional medical tests. What is more, even if maternity care given to the surrogate is covered by the NHS, fertility treatments such as insemination or in vitro fertilisation during surrogacy arrangements are not yet covered by the NHS for same-sex couples and single parents. Out of the 30 families I interviewed, 22 pursued gestational rather than traditional surrogacy arrangements, which meant that two women helped them, a surrogate and an egg donor. None of those 22 families received any NHS funding and they all used commercial fertility clinics for insemination, in vitro fertilisation and other fertility treatments. This more than doubled the costs, as IVF expenses alone amounted to almost £14,000 in some cases. Given that multiple fertility treatments were often necessary, those costs frequently grew from the initial total of £27,000 for a gestational surrogacy arrangement to a total of £50,000 or even £60,000. For this reason, all of the families I interviewed had average annual household incomes above the UK average of £32,300 (Office for National Statistics 2022). Therefore, one of the currently relevant issues Alan mentions is 'attaining an equality between surrogacy journeys and traditional parenthood' and overcoming the inequality due to 'differential prices for surrogacy journeys relative to non-surrogacy clinic journeys'.

These issues are also accompanied by inequalities in law and employment benefits, according to Alan. For example, as a surrogacy parent one is eligible for adoption leave. However, self-employed people are not eligible for adoption leave.

Within SUK, Alan also plans to campaign against the inequality resulting from double gamete donations. Surrogacy in the UK requires that one of the intended parents is biologically related to the prospective child. However, this is not always possible, due to sexuality, fertility, transgender status or disability. As a result, people seeking surrogacy are often deemed ineligible. On the other hand, in heterosexual routes to parenthood through IVF, double gamete donation is legal.

In 2023 Alan was one of eight activists – all members or allies of Surrogacy UK – who came together to establish the Surrogacy UK Foundation, the UK's first surrogacy charity. The foundation exists to 'advance the education of the public about surrogacy and, in particular, approaches to surrogacy that are ethical and safeguard the interests of all parties' and is further evidence of the intersection between activism and reproductive justice. Alan's hope is that the charity will help engender social acceptance of both surrogacy and LGBTQ+ parenting, and support the welfare and wellbeing of people born through surrogacy, like his son.

Similarly to the trans dad Freddy, introduced earlier in this chapter, Alan went through a process of consciousness change (Smietana 2019), which enabled him to imagine that being LGBTQ+ and having children are not mutually exclusive or contradictory. Like Richard, the gay dad through international surrogacy, Alan first reached out to LGBTQ+ and surrogacy charities and organisations in order to explore what parenting options he and his husband had. And like all the other parent-activists whose accounts are discussed in this chapter, he gradually became involved in campaigning for LGBTQ+ family rights, as he saw from his own experience that it was needed.

Conclusion

The reproductive life stories of five LGBTQ+ parent-activists in the UK, discussed in this chapter, are not only stories of their reproductive lives but also stories of their activism. They represent many patterns I found in my broader study of 30 families created by gay men through surrogacy in the UK. This twofold character – reproductive and activist at once – makes them similar to the 'procreation stories' discussed by Faye Ginsburg (1989) in her research with abortion activists in the US, even if there are important differences between the two. This does not mean that all LGBTQ+ parents become activists. However, both in their personal journeys to parenthood and in their activism, all five parent-activists have actively worked against traditional social norms of kinship and gender. Such norms have been deeply ingrained, even in the relatively progressive social and legal context of the UK, which has become increasingly supportive for LGBTQ+ families. All five parent-activists talk about their own lack of knowledge about their parenting options at the beginning of their journeys, due to which they contacted communities and families formed by LGBTQ+ parents, many of whom were activists. Likewise, not all the gay fathers I interviewed in the UK, in the 30 families created through surrogacy, were activists, but all of them were part of the broader UK or international surrogacy communities, and all of them without exception had attended activist and community events for LGBTQ+ families, as part of their pathway to parenthood. This points to the crucial importance that activism, community building and awareness raising have for family formation by LGBTQ+ people.

The five parent-activists featured in this chapter discussed several barriers to LGBTQ+ family formation. Over the last two decades, such barriers have been diminishing and evolving towards a more inclusive situation for LGBTQ+ parent families in the UK. However, many barriers still persist. The first issue was the lack of social awareness of alternative routes to parenthood and LGBTQ+ parent families, whether in gender clinics (Freddy), workplace and activities for parents with babies (Richard) or broader society, including LGBTQ+ people themselves (Alan). The second challenge lies in legislation that continues to have several gaps, as increasingly inclusive as it is: registering the person who gives birth as a mother on the birth certificate (Freddy), the lower status of home insemination as compared to insemination in fertility clinics and its implications for birth certificates (Erika), the lengthy and complex process of obtaining parental orders following surrogacy (Richard, Alan), as well as the character of employment benefits that is frequently limited by gender and class (Richard, Alan). Legislative gaps are also linked to the third issue the parent-activists mentioned: the heteronormativity of public healthcare, based on the medical definition of infertility, and the resulting unaffordability of fertility treatments for many lesbian (Jackie) and gay (Alan) intended parents.

Some of the barriers have been overcome. The parent-activists observed a gradual change in social awareness of LGBTQ+ parent families and in legislation, as well as the growing inclusion of LGBTQ+ people in adoption agencies and fertility clinics. Some of the issues have subsided thanks to the work undertaken by the parent-activists themselves: for example, the difficulty in finding known donors for home insemination has been at least partly addressed thanks to organisations such as Pride Angel (Erika). Yet a lot is still to be done to achieve queer reproductive justice where 'identifying as LGBTQ should not place exceptional demands or restrictions upon one's access to reproductive care and services', as we argued with Charis Thompson and France Winddance Twine (Smietana et al. 2018, 214).

One limitation of this chapter is that among the parent-activists whose accounts are discussed, reproductive technologies and practices such as surrogacy, IVF and artificial insemination have been used most widely, followed by adoption. However, there is little discussion of options such as coparenting with friends, or of queer family configurations with more than two parents or caregivers. The founder of Pride Angel, Erika Tranfield, does highlight the existence of such options. However, the event did not include a parent-activist representing this route to family formation. In particular, following the 2021 event that gave rise to this chapter, groups such as Queer Platonic Co-parenting (2024) have emerged, and any future discussions of queer families and kinships should include their voices, which may provide alternatives to the nuclear family and couple logic. In doing this and inviting as many diverse queer and trans families to the table, we 'refuse to renaturalize or valorize certain forms of reproduction over others' (Mamo 2018, 24).

Acknowledgements

The research was funded by the Wellcome Trust, UK (Grant no. 209829/Z/17/Z), as well as the Centre for Research in the Arts, Social Sciences and Humanities (CRASSH) and the lgbtQ+@cam programme at the University of Cambridge. The paper was written with further support from the Spanish Ministry of Science and Innovation (Grant PID2020–112692RB-C21/AEI/10.13039/501100011033). I owe my gratitude for inspiration, collaboration and support in writing this chapter to the volume editors, Natasha Tanna, Hakan Sandal-Wilson and Abeyamí Ortega Domínguez, as well as to the speakers in the event that forms the basis for this chapter: Jackie Fernandez, Freddy McConnell, Erika Tranfield, Alan White and Richard.

References

Bednarek, Julia, Piotr Laskowski, Sebastian Matuszewski, Łukasz Mikołajewski and Michał Sobczak (eds). 2022. *Cała Siła, Jaką Czerpię Na Życie: Świadectwa, relacje, pamiętniki osób LGBTQ+*. Kraków: Karakter.

Berkowitz, Dana. 2007. 'A sociohistorical analysis of gay men's procreative consciousness', *Journal of GLBT Family Studies* 3(2–3): 157–90. https://doi.org/10.1300/J461v03n02_07.

Creaction. 2021. 'Creative critical interventions for social justice'. Institute of Advanced Studies, UCL. Accessed 13 September 2024. https://www.ucl.ac.uk/institute-of-advanced-studies/news/2021/apr/creaction-creative-critical-interventions-social-justice.

Cromer, Risa, Lea Taragin-Zeller and Sarah Franklin (eds). 2024. 'Reproductive righteousness and the new right extremism: Global feminist perspectives', *Women's Studies International Forum* 105(July–August). Accessed 3 June 2025. https://www.sciencedirect.com/special-issue/10X6JJCCH3R.

Current Issues for Queer and Trans Families: Activist Roundtable. 2021. An online event convened within the research network 'Global conversations towards queer social justice', at the University of Cambridge on 25 November 2021. Accessed 4 November 2024. https://www.crassh.cam.ac.uk/events/29920/.

Department of Health and Social Care (with Maria Caulfield). 2023. 'IVF law change to benefit couples with fertility issues'. Accessed 31 October 2024. https://www.gov.uk/government/news/ivf-law-change-to-benefit-couples-with-fertility-issues.

Ginsburg, Faye. 1989. *Contested Lives: The abortion debate in an American community*. Berkeley: University of California Press.

'Global conversations towards queer social justice'. 2021. Research network and online event series, Centre for Research in the Arts, Social Sciences and Humanities, University of Cambridge (2021–2). Accessed 3 June 2025. https://www.crassh.cam.ac.uk/research/networks/global-conversations-towards-queer-social-justice-2021-22/.

Golombok, Susan. 2015. *Modern Families: Parents and children in new family forms*. Cambridge: Cambridge University Press.

Law Commission. 2023. 'Surrogacy laws to be overhauled under new reforms: Benefitting the child, surrogate and intended parents'. 29 March. Accessed 3 November 2024. https://lawcom.gov.uk/surrogacy-laws-to-be-overhauled-under-new-reforms-benefitting-the-child-surrogate-and-intended-parents/.

Mamo, Laura. 2018. 'Queering reproduction in transnational bio-economies', *Reproductive Biomedicine & Society Online* 7: 24–32. https://doi.org/10.1016/j.rbms.2018.10.008.

Methods in Question: Epistemologies of Gender and Sexuality. 2018. Accessed 31 October 2024. https://methodsinquestion.co.uk/.

New Family Social. 2023. '1 in 5 adoptions in England to same-sex couples'. Accessed 23 September 2025. https://newfamilysocial.org.uk/General-News/13281613.

Office for National Statistics. 2022. 'Average household income, UK: Financial year ending 2022'. Accessed 5 August 2025. https://tinyurl.com/ycxmupkb.

Pralat, Robert. 2018. 'More natural does not equal more normal: Lesbian, gay, and bisexual people's views about different pathways to parenthood', *Journal of Family Issues* 39(18). https://doi.org/10.1177/0192513X18810951.

Queer Platonic Co-parenting. 2024. An Instagram community that also holds regular in-person events in the UK. Accessed 4 November 2024. https://www.instagram.com/queerplatonicc oparenting/?hl=en.

Ross, Loretta and Rickie Solinger. 2017. *Reproductive Justice: An introduction*. Berkeley: University of California Press.

Sandal-Wilson, Hakan and Natasha Tanna. 2020. 'The politics of writing in and with crises: A conversation with Dr Natasha Tanna' [blog post]. *Methods in Question*. Accessed 31 October 2024. https://methodsinquestion.co.uk/blog/f/the-politics-of-writing-in-and-with-crisis.

Schorscher-Pecu, Ana. 2021. 'Lesbian Couple Takes CCG to Court over IVF Discrimination', *BioNews* 1121, 15 November. Accessed 3 June 2025. https://www.progress.org.uk/lesbi an-couple-takes-ccg-to-court-over-ivf-discrimination/.

Sistersong. 2007. 'Women of color reproductive health collective and the pro-choice public education project', *Reproductive Justice Briefing Book: A primer on reproductive justice and social change*. Accessed 6 July 2025. https://www.protectchoice.org/downloads/ Reproductive%20Justice%20Briefing%20Book.pdf.

Smietana, Marcin. 2019. 'Procreative consciousness in a global market: Gay men's paths to surrogacy in the US', *Reproductive Biomedicine and Society* 7(November): 101–11. https://doi.org/10.1016/j.rbms.2019.03.001.

Smietana, Marcin. 2024. 'Unreproductive citizenship: Social sterilization of queer and trans people in Poland', *Women's Studies International Forum*, special issue, 'Reproductive righteousness and the New Right extremism: Global feminist perspectives', edited by Risa Cromer, Lea Taragin-Zeller and Sarah Franklin, 105(July–August). https://doi.org/10.1016/j.wsif.2024.102948.

Smietana, Marcin. 2025. 'Queer calculations: spreadsheet fertility and British gay men's reproductive projects'. In *The New Reproductive Order: Technology, fertility, and social change around the globe*, edited by Sarah Franklin and Marcia Inhorn, 103–22. New York: New York University Press.

Smietana, Marcin, Charis Thompson and France Winddance Twine (eds). 2018. 'Making and breaking families: Reading queer reproductions, stratified reproduction and reproductive justice together'. *Reproductive Biomedicine and Society Online*, 7(Nov). https://doi.org/10.1016/j.rbms.2018.11.001.

Smietana, Marcin and France Winddance Twine. 2022. 'Queer decisions: Racial matching and stigma management among gay male intended parents', *International Journal of Comparative Sociology* 63(5–6): 324–44. https://doi.org/10.1177/00207152221102837.

Twine, France Winddance. 2010. *A White Side of Black Britain: Interracial intimacy and racial literacy*. Durham, NC: Duke University Press.

Weeks, Jeffrey. 2017. *Sex, Politics and Society: The regulation of sexuality since 1800*, 4th edition. London: Routledge. https://doi.org/10.4324/9781315161525.

Part III

Paradox and parody: the politics of positionality and relationality

5
Notes on lying

Mathelinda Nabugodi

When do you begin to lie?

My education has been a history of learning to lie. It begins with encounters with strangers. *Where are you from?* Sweden. *Yes, but where do you* ***come*** *from?* Malmö. Sweden's third largest city. Capital of Skåne, Sweden's southernmost province, just across the Öresund strait from Copenhagen – when I was growing up the bridge connecting the two had not yet been built. *OK, but where are you* ***really*** *from?* That *really* signals dissatisfaction. My interlocutor, seeing my skin colour, the shape of my nose, my lips, the texture of my hair, is not pleased with 'Sweden' for an answer. A country of blond people. Slim hips, thin noses, straight tresses. *Where are you really from?* For years I tried to answer honestly. Well, I'm born in Minsk, in Belarus, then part of the Soviet Union … We moved to Sweden when I was four. *But,* the interlocutor insists, *where are you* ***really*** *from?* Meaning: why are you Black? I grew up hearing this question. I soon learnt that whichever interlocutor would not be satisfied until I named an African country. Doesn't matter which one. My father's from Angola. I'm half Ethiopian. I was born in Senegal. My family is from South Africa. None of which is true. Yet it was the easiest way to stop the questioning. The ease made me bolder. I'm from California. Or Harlem, New York. I'm Brazilian. I was born in Jamaica. Egypt. Afghanistan? Kenya! Then I got tired. *Where are you from?* I just fell down from the moon.

One of the reasons why I moved to the UK was because I wanted to escape the question of where I'm from. I thought that living in a country with an erstwhile empire on the African continent and a larger Black diaspora would make it **easier** to blend in. To come from **here**. But the question has haunted me in the UK as well. *Where are you from? Really from?* Sometimes followed by: *Go back to where you came from!*

At other times, it's more subtle: *What's your name?* Mathelinda. *Where is it from?* Oooooh, Africa! (Enjoy the feigned surprise.) *What does it mean?* Well, in Spanish *linda* means beautiful, so I guess it kind of means that maths is beautiful. *Yes, but African names have such beautiful meanings.* It is an English name. It is the name that the British colonisers gave my grandmother. *Mathelinda? But it's so long? Don't you have a short form … Mattie? Lindy?* I have no patience with this. Anywhere else but here, sure. But certainly not here. I've googled the name and found: **one** woman born in Alabama in the nineteenth century. **One** Ugandan woman living in New York today. And myself. But the truth is that my grandmother would never have been named Mathelinda had it not been for the British Empire. And so I have no patience with British people stumbling over my name. *Mathelinda? Is that with t or th?* I don't mind. And that is true.

Or is it?

***

We're in a coffee shop. It's named after a literary character, need I say which one? It's corporate, global, distressed chic. Choices are over-individualised. All I want is a coffee, but I need to answer a veritable questionnaire about cup size, milk type, bean origin, froth density. Topped off with *What's your name?* Mathelinda. *Matilda?* **Ma**the**li**nda. *Madeleine?* Mathe**linda**. *Belinda?* In the end, I choose a coffee shop name. Sarah. A tall soy latte for Sarah, please. House roast. No sugar. This solves the issue, except when I'm with someone who knows me, when naming myself Sarah becomes awkward. Caught in my lie. Yet my coffee shop name is easy enough to justify to friends so I continue carrying it around – like a badge of honour – until the day when I encountered a barista who wants to know whether it's Sarah with or without an 'h' at the end. No matter, I say. *No, but it's really important to get it right*, she insists. Then it's Sarah with an 'h', I reply. Afterwards, the friend I'm with tells me that, if I were to be a Sarah, she'd envisage me as a Sara without an 'h'. We discuss the difference between Sarah and Sara. I stop calling myself Sara(h).

Or do I?

***

My coffee shop name is a lie, but how different is it from my academic research expertise lie? In the fifteen years – my entire adult life – that I've spent at university, I've learnt to write in a style that is disinterested and authoritative, unmoved by personal prejudices or bugbears. In research statements, articles and conference presentations, I justify my work in objective terms, arguing that it is necessary and important because it makes an original contribution to existing knowledge about Romanticism. But there is something dishonest about all of this: like naming myself Sarah for convenience, devoting myself to critical appreciation of Romantic poetry purposefully obscures what matters most, to me, intimately: the reason why I bother to spend hours with the words of long-dead poets, many of whom I would no doubt find unbearable in person. So why do I do it? Well, for me, with the education that I have had (bearing in mind imperial residues of cultural capital and high art), British Romantic poetry has symbolised poetry *par excellence*. Philosophical, complex, boring. White, male, stale. In mastering this, I can master anything. First we take the poets, then we take the world.

In short: I'm proving something. To myself. To others. But regardless of how much I might have strived for mastery over the canon, and impersonal objectivity in my critical analysis, a lifetime inhabiting my particular body – of navigating the social situations, symbolised by the incessant *where are you from?* – will invariably have left a mark on my thinking: I might be an expert on dead White poets, but my experience as a woman of colour affects my reading of their work – not least because I am ever-again positioned as an outsider in the majority-White society that reveres these works as part of its canon and history. That's the true significance of the question. Whoever asks me *Where are you from?* also implicitly states that ***You** are not from here. You **do not** belong here. **I** do and **I** have the **right** to demand that you render up an account of yourself.*

***

Render up an account of yourself. This is also the demand of peer review. By way of rejecting this demand – the demand of anonymous judgement, of scholarly rigour, of impersonal objectivity – my research has taken an autobiographical turn. Of course, I can ground it rigorously and methodically in imposing terms: auto-theory; auto-ethnography; critical fabulation; feminist speculation; fugitive epistemology; creative non-fiction, but above all, for me, the autobiographical has offered a route to resistance. One of the key premises of scholarship is that we as scholars be honest, tell the truth, present real findings from the archive or the fieldwork. Substantive facts and not a handful of anecdotes that we just invented on the go. Yet so much of Western thought has been produced in bad faith: philosophers, statesmen, natural scientists, biologists, theologians, artists and others have offered spurious arguments to prove the inferiority of non-European peoples and cultures and, in so doing, have justified colonial violence, enslavement and genocide. If we accept that academic disciplines are profoundly implicated in the epistemologies of White supremacism that underpinned European empires, then any attempt to achieve epistemic justice in research requires us to rethink its premises from the ground up. Including the demand for honesty and truthfulness.

The demand to be truthful in academic writing is related to the even more fundamental concept of objectivity – the illusion that the researcher is disinterested and disembodied: a pure intellect unmoored from their body or contemporary politics. Of course, we now know that this seemingly 'neutral' position is in fact the stance of a European gentleman of independent means and, moreover, that this very neutrality has served to discredit non-European and non-heteromasculinist knowledge practices. From that perspective, turning to the personal offers a way of challenging the objectivity of 'objectivity'. Moreover, it enables us to ground our intellectual labour in our embodied, racialised, sexed being in the world.

Or does it?

In talking about the personal, the private, the intimate (in short, about identity politics) from my position as a Black woman, I conform to certain prejudices about women and people of colour: that we only have expertise in our own experience. We do not know anything other than what it's like to be ourselves. Our research is navel-gazing 'me-search'. And while it's currently exotic enough to be admitted into an academy hungry for decolonisation and diversification, it is not objective enough to be received as serious scholarship. So I wonder, does my autobiographical turn undermine the work that I hope to do?

***

Either way, even when research takes an autobiographical turn, it doesn't mean that the lying stops. From Instagram to the CV – do we not lie all the time? Lying is perhaps too harsh a term; let's say we embellish the truth. After all, as anyone trained in the canon of autobiography has been taught to know: the need to tell a story drives the arrangement of factual details. Of how we tell a life. As soon as you set pen to paper, or fingers to keyboard, narrative form enters the picture. Literary models determine how we write a life; the spare backbone of historical fact becomes covered in the voluptuous flesh of imaginative storytelling. Paul de Man wrote about this, years before I was born, in an essay called 'Autobiography as de-facement'. He is, by the way, another professional liar: who stripped himself of his past writing for a Nazi-sympathising newspaper in World War II Belgium, who feigned having a PhD to land his first job at Harvard.

Forget Paul de Man. I want to come at this from another perspective. Rather than the distortion inherent in *any* literary endeavour, I want to speak about lying as a specific mode of Black resistance. In the slave societies of the Americas, pretending to be too stupid to understand, too stupid to talk properly, too stupid to read, were tricks used to outwit enslavers. Can I bring that mode of resistance into my own reading and writing practice? Doing so would resonate with other modes of resisting the epistemological structures that oppress us. Resistances voiced by feminists, Indigenous, queer and other radicals, fed up with the narrow-mindedness of academic knowledge production. Take, for instance, Édouard Glissant's concept of opacity (1997). This is an act of resistance to European colonialism, whose extractive logics include the desire to know the world of the Other, to make it perfectly translatable into European epistemic structures. A translation without residue. Against this, Glissant promotes the opacity of the Caribbean condition: embracing that which the coloniser cannot fathom.

***

This is nothing new. My research is on British Romanticism. The decades around 1800, a time when Britain was convulsed with debates about the rights and wrongs of slavery, which would culminate in the Abolition of the Slave Trade Act 1807. The slave trade, mind, not slavery as a system. Nonetheless, if you read accounts of interracial encounters from that period, you will find a litany of complaints about how hard it is to decipher Black behaviour. 'It is not an easy matter to trace with an unerring pencil the true character and dispositions of the negro', the travel writer John Stewart complained in an account of Jamaica published in 1808, 'they are often so ambiguous and disguised' (Stewart 1808, 235). They're lying, and he knows it. Lying not as a mark of dishonesty and failing morals, but rather as an emblem of defiance. *You think you see me, but you don't*. From the very beginnings of New World slavery, Black people have resorted to lying to assert their humanity in the face of a system that denied it. Dissimulation is a way of getting one up on your oppressor. No wonder the tone of exasperation among the White observers who tried to pin down what they heard and saw.

With this in mind, I want to ask: if one of the key premises of Western knowledge is that it be known in its truthfulness, is it ok to lie?

Prima facie, yes. By lying, I protect myself from intrusive questioning (*Where do you come from? What's your name?*). I protect myself from my personal investments, separating my intellectual self from the professional work. But also, and more importantly, I protect myself from the academy itself. Because its condition for entry is that the budding academic takes up a position that is rigorous, objective, impersonal, disinterested, authoritative and so on and so on: a position historically derived from the perspective of White, European, well-off men who could afford to distance themselves from their private, messy selves. By following in their footsteps, I am forcing myself into a position of deception. I lie to myself. Which is to say that I can either deceive myself (which I've been doing throughout the long years of undergraduate and graduate study) or I can deceive the disciplined institution (which is where I am now).

So I lie. In my academic work, I lie.

Is that true?

***

Who cares about 'my truth'? No, I don't want to fall into the trap of the personal. The trap that locks women and people of colour into only talking about ourselves and our lived experience of discrimination, as if that's the only thing we know. I do know other things, too, for example I know a lot about eighteenth-century literature, a literature that was written as White supremacist violence exploded exponentially around the globe. But this literature does not concern itself with that, or only marginally so. Instead, sincerity and sentiment are its hallmarks. Pale, trembling heroines who spend half the novel in a fainting fit. Dashing heroes with £10,000 a year and a pistol in their pocket, ever ready to fight a duel for the imaginary honour of his beloved. Or poets moodily brooding over sublime mountains and stormy seas, everything they see as an emblem for the grandeur of their own soul. All these are tokens of sincerity, and contribute to the cultural landscape in which we find ourselves. Of course it is not ok to lie when telling a sob story about your own sufferings!

To get to grips with the intersection of race and sincerity, I want to close with a poem. It is a sonnet by Charlotte Smith, called 'The Captive Escaped in the Wilds of America. Addressed to the Hon. Mrs. O'Neill':

> If, by his torturing, savage foes untraced,
>   The breathless Captive gain some trackless glade,
> Yet hears the war-whoop howl along the waste.
>   And dreads the reptile-monsters of the shade;

The giant reeds that murmur round the flood,
    Seem to conceal some hideous form beneath;
And every hollow blast that shakes the wood,
    Speaks to his trembling heart of woe and death.
With horror fraught, and desolate dismay,
    On such a wanderer falls the starless night;
But if, far streaming, a propitious ray
    Leads to some amicable fort his sight,
He hails the beam benign that guides his way,
    As I, my Harriet, bless thy friendship's cheering light.

The sonnet was published in 1784, three years before the foundation of the Society for the Abolition of the Slave Trade that first launched an organised campaign against slavery. That's one reason why it differs from the wave of abolitionist poetry that followed in the 1790s – the latter was a commercially successful genre that drew on sentimental conventions to stir sympathy for the poor, benighted slaves, who were depicted kneeling, chained, beaten, torn from family and home. *Am I not a man and a brother?* the kneeling figure on the Wedgwood medallion beseeches – a plea intended to solicit the answer 'yes'. Yet the very formulation puts the man's humanity into question. It opens up the option of saying no: *No, you are not my brother. No, you are not a man.*

So it is with much abolitionist work of the 1790s. While the intentions might be good, its underlying imaginary cannot overcome its doubts about whether Africans are truly human, 'like us'. That is why this rhetoric is so rife with visions of extreme anti-Black violence: reports of people being boiled alive, dismembered, flayed, covered with molasses and left to the ants … While factually accurate, there is an uncanny salaciousness, a disturbing sense of relish, in the facility with which these images are reproduced and circulate. In them, the Black body becomes the container for envisaging pain beyond what a mortal body can stand – breaking into something suprahuman in its debasement. *No, you are not my brother and that's why I enjoy seeing you writhe in pain.*

This sonnet is different. Smith imagines herself in the body of the 'captive' who escapes the plantation and flees into the bush. Word choices underpin her politics – by calling the enslaved person a captive, she does not emphasise their race, but their unjust treatment, while the term savage (normally reserved for racially othered people) is here used for White enslavers. The choice of 'captive' also anticipates the poet's identification with the escapee in the final line of the poem ('As I …'), because Charlotte Smith, too, saw herself as a captive.

Born to a genteel household with a spendthrift father, she was forced to marry at the age of fifteen, in part to help pay her father's debts. Her husband, Benjamin Smith, had money – loads of money – blood money – derived from the slave trade and plantations on Barbados. Married against her will to a slaveholder, Charlotte Smith saw her own marriage as personal slavery. While the abolitionist movement was fuelled by White British women – spurred by sentiment, female delicacy, sexual jealousy and an opportunity to gain political agency – Smith's work has a peculiar resonance, because she saw herself in the enslaved. That was 'her truth'. In good faith, perhaps. Possibly. But what do I make of her good faith if it didn't prevent her from discarding the captive's flight as soon as she had fulfilled her creative aims? She spends thirteen lines imagining what it feels like to run towards freedom through a dangerous tropical nightscape, only to enliven a trite remark on friendship. The about-face is grotesque.

Is she being for real? Does she sincerely believe her experience of friendship to be akin to an escaped captive's experience of freedom?

Or is it a neatly dramatic image for a polite compliment to Mrs Harriet O'Neill? A ruse, a lie?

Does it matter? If so, tell me why.

References

De Man, Paul. 1984. 'Auto-biography as de-facement'. In *The Rhetoric of Romanticism*, 67–81. New York: Columbia University Press.

Glissant, Édouard. 1997. *Poetics of Relation*, translated by Betsy Wing. Ann Arbor: University of Michigan Press.

Smith, Charlotte. 1984. 'The captive escaped in the wilds of America: Addressed to the Hon. Mrs. O'Neill', *Elegiac Sonnets* (1784), reproduced in *The Poems of Charlotte Smith*, edited by Stuart Curran, 50. New York: Oxford University Press.

Stewart, John. 1808. *An Account of Jamaica, and its Inhabitants*. London: Longman, Hurst, Rees and Orme.

6

Queer Mediterranean futures: an {uneventful} performative text

Anna T.

Academic article abstract

'______________ _____: A study on the use of the __________ in ________ _____ through the comparison of two projects' published on __________ & ________, Taylor & Francine Online

Keywords: qualitative, _____, __________, minority, _______

Abstract

This article presents two case studies of two different self-identifying 'queer-feminist projects'; _______ and ________. Based in different countries, with a different history and lifespan, the two were chosen as they carry the same label and share similar mission statements. They are both in ______-______ countries, with similarly diverse demographics in terms of age, religious backgrounds, ethnicities, and GDP. ________ began as a squat living project and social space in an urban centre and later transformed into a community project at the edge of the city recently hosting refugees, while _______ has always been by the sea in the outskirts of a small settlement on an island catering to both locals and foreigners. Their different profiles but similar membership numbers offer an ideal setting for comparisons. As is the case in many queer-feminist spaces, more people identify as ________, or ____________ and are more prone to be _______ and in support of the __________ __ _______ ___ ______ than their non-queer-feminist counterparts. The research conducted over a period of six months in late 2022 is a qualitative study with three _____ _______ persons from ________ and four from _______ carried through in-person and over video conferencing interviews.

Dr Mia DeDixeris (she, her) Written on December 2nd, 2022, Prepublication Notes Document.

This, dear reader, is an attempt at exploring something while opacifying aspects of it due to discomfort, a sense of protection, and methodology borrowing from writer and poet Édouard Glissant. Glissant proposed opacity as the only precondition for relationality: a bottom up agential use of language by oppressed people who were historically forced to be transparent (Glissant 1997). It also opens up the space for you to project and fill in the gaps in ways that reflect your experiences. Academic tradition sees unfinishedness, error and playfulness as antithetical to its aims and style. Here, I'm looking at what these elements can offer to a volume on social justice by presenting a ~~fictional~~ archive of a collective focused on social justice interspersed with unfinished thoughts and meta-commentary pondering on what such processes could look like in the Mediterranean ~~in the future~~.

Borrowing the notion of 'uneventfulness' from Maria Mayerchyk and Olga Plakhotnik (2021) to think of this experimental essay as both comprised of banal archival documents and in the postcolonial and anti-capitalist (see 'unproductive') way that the authors use it in[1] *I feel I have to clarify my positionality. I am from Greece, living in Austria for many years at this point, having migrated to two other countries before that. I am a first gen artist and academic from a lower-middle-class family from various areas in the Aegean sea.*

Similarly to Mayerchyk and Plakhotnik, my positionality is in some respects one of Central Europe, in others located within an Anglo universe, and in others still it's very much within Southeastern Europe, the Balkans and the Mediterranean. The context is, here too, postcolonial (in this case referring to the Ottoman Empire) though there are significant differences to the Western post/decolonial paradigm (semi-periphery's conditions, irredentism/s, the ongoing situation in the Near and Middle East).

Throughout this project I ~~enact~~ perform a type of archive, a regular archive of the past within the fictional parameters set in the year 2064, and

[1] Uneventful here means that the documents themselves are banal, often administrative documents, some with short life spans. It also refers to the use of the term 'uneventful feminism' borrowed from Maria Mayerchyk and Olga Plakhotnik to mean feminism which pursues both anti-nationalist and anti-colonial agendas (2021, 122). Their analysis focuses on small artivist collectives that create small events that activate 'uneventfulness, anonymity, and unsuccessfulness (opposing the capitalist meaning of success)' (2021, 126).

an archive of the past, present and future in real life. Archives are often the sites of reflections on past pedagogies and ethos and the editorial processes that go into bringing them to light are testament to the lens of the present.

I put together this collection drawing from personal experiences, texts, artworks and discussions that have inspired me. In some ways, though it makes me uncomfortable due to the vast differences, it has similarities with Saidiya Hartman's 'critical fabulations' method. Whereas she looks to bring out stories from the past, filling gaps in the archive, I am speaking from what is at present the future, looking at what will be in the future the past, narrating it and commenting on it with today's knowledge trying to figure out the big and small shifts in ontological understandings and epistemological approaches. There are also gaps in this future archive which need to remain such. Through banality, uneventfulness and relationality, I stay away from spectacles of violence, even though many are implied and referred to. Banality and uneventfulness also reflect the realities of long-term activist practice and community-building that undergirds what is often more 'spectacular' coverage of activist organising – both in its successes and failures – in media coverage.

Passage of بينيلوبي

I don't know when this took place, but it's safe to assume it was well before any of our times. I've heard the story many times, from various people, some of whom are no longer with us. Here's how I remember it: She sailed by herself from Al Hoceima to Beirut, more than 2,600 miles in 39 days. She meant to go there to change her documents, itself the result of a two-year-long journey. She meant for the journey to be carbon neutral and preferably exclusively wind- and sun-powered. Initially she thought she would share the journey with others, but due to a variety of reasons she had to do it solo and used this time as a meditative journey, to finish the painful, stressful and unkind one she had set out on two years earlier. She prepared with the help of Mariana and Nenet and borrowed Aya's friend's pickup truck (lovingly named 'Datsun') over the course of a week and stocked up on fresh produce (some of which she would vacuum-bag), canned goods and grains. The crowdfunding campaign we had launched earlier that year allowed her to stock up on supplies, petrol (she could only afford an old kayık), and install higher wattage soft panels with a new series of batteries from ethically-sourced materials.

That would be the first time she would sail such a distance from West to East. She had sailed parts of it during different MIEM |Mediterranean

Interventionist Environmental Movement| campaigns and she was familiar with many of the conditions, though she always had a crew of four at least. She would make landfall in approximately 30 days, according to her initial calculations and then would sail to join us. The island was itself in transition, being part of an archipelago that had only recently become independent and had opened its borders, doing away with the violence of the coast guard after the EU agency dissolved with the union which buckled under the weight of explicit fascism.

The contraste |winds| at the beginning of her journey were bothersome, yet familiar and expected. People kept in touch, checking in with her over the internet and radio, so for the first six days or so, despite the little sleep, she felt energised by the support everyone showed her. She kept the kayık log and her audio diary tirelessly. She also sent us long voice texts usually during the night watch. She spent her time listening to our voice messages, audiobooks and sometimes old podcast episodes. She had promised herself to stop holding on to things that she didn't feel connected to anymore. I guess that was part of the journey. So she listened to podcasts she had downloaded months or years earlier, so she could clear out her device. Some were interesting, she gave me synopses often in her quiet night-watch voice messages. Most felt odd to her, irrelevant even. They must have been topical when she downloaded them but she couldn't remember anymore what their appeal had been. She also took up knitting again. She would randomly text, asking if I like yellow, orange and light blue, or any other combo of the yarn she had bought before leaving. If she didn't like it she would undo and redo it the next day. Different colour combos, or a different function altogether (coasters were the easiest).

She moored in a small leeward spot in the port of Carthage, for three days, while a strong sirocco blew with only small breaks.

She moored in Lampeduża for two nights and reunited with Chkristophfer and Renata |Germanic volunteers against Frontex and the EU's policies|. They caught up around the fire.

She saw a whale breach in the distance and sent me a shaky video, to celebrate the sighting together.

Her anchor dragged, so she motored a few miles and got a mooring in the port of Alexandria, where she was able to catch up on her sleep. She was able to get more fresh foods and go by the carenaggio to get impeller spares, as the ones she had fitted before setting off were making strange sounds and she saw they were wearing out fast.

She collected trash throughout her passage and recycled/threw it away whenever she made landfall.

Somewhere a harbourmaster was extremely rude and shamed her for her accent.

She was ushered by dolphins for several days in a row, once by one of these megapods that were becoming more frequent encounters in the Med in those days.

The bora and meltem |Mediterranean/Aegean winds| boosted the final part of the passage, that was, by that time, exhausting. With the wind on her beam she sailed the final leg at 7–8 kn. She could smell the thyme, the sage and the olive trees.

The autopilot drive, that connected to the rudder, failed on day 37, so the last two days were exclusively hand steering. She was sore but calm. The calm one is when they are too exhausted to react elsewise. The calm one is when they can see the finishing line. بينيلوبي would finally get to come home to herself, before she joined us, arriving in the home we had made for her in anticipation of her arrival.

Handwritten on paper by anonymous, date unknown.

The collective, like the place itself, had their own accounts of oral tradition and lore. Journeys of self-actualisation, of solidarity and overcoming adversity, especially ones that involve the sea have long been part of the cultures of the basin. Unlike the ancient epics or modern literature where a hero's journey is connected to ideas of nationhood, victory, or the patriarchy, here I wonder what oral tradition, one that involves nautical tradition and multiple cultures, could do for the visibility and depathologisation of queer and trans journeys. How would the (re)telling of stories impact audiences? How would it reshape the folk imagination land- and sea-scape? What would it mean to think of transitioning as nostos and the journey as a maritime one?

Hospitality and Culture Working Group

Ğa sas insanlar,
We call you (members and supporters) to action, fundraising and showing solidarity.

An earthquake is predicted for some time in the next two weeks, in the wider region of P. It would be wise to prepare additional dwellings as it is almost certain that we will have an influx of musafir and refugees (human and nonhuman) from the low elevation coastal villages and neighbouring islands. We remind you that the medicane season is predicted to begin in six weeks.

To accommodate persons in need from the upcoming crisis, and any other (the pyroseason |A neologism (mine) referring to the season of arson attacks that destroy and eventually declassify forest areas as forest and allow development as well as the fires that start as a result of draughts and pollution| isn't nearly over), we would like to up our emergency hospitality capacity and our permanent dwellings and expand the village towards the hills. Our Habitat Working Group of architects, artists, builders, electrologists, engineers, environmentalists, pedagogues, phytologists and psychologists has been working on the plans for over two years (for the permanent dwellings) but we need to hurry in order to have them move-in ready in the next few weeks and set up the emergency hospitality dwellings right after. The printers are ready and the mods are being constructed.

We need to:

- raise berde |money| to have cash and ecoin available for them,
- enlist nonorganic and organic translators and admin assistants to help with paperwork,
- collect season-appropriate clothes (for fall/winter),
- collect beddings,
- collect ethical food preserves donations,
- baby food and green diapers,
- cat and dog food (low CO_2) and eco litter.

Locals are ready for the solpal |solar panels| installation. The expansion of our kelp culture is still behind but this is not something that should be sped up.

Our ergo/therapists, counsellors, legal assistants, medics and lesonotsardo |neologism meaning 'school' based on Kaliarda| teachers are ready to help in indabuever |whatever from Cypriot Greek 'indabu' meaning 'what'| way possible and if need be we will hire externals so that no one will have to work shifts longer than five hours a day.

We call on berdetzoudes[2] |Neologism based on Kaliarda meaning 'moneyed'| and paralii |Bulgarian root to mean 'wealthy'| to support by sharing their wealth at 3:{0=:atY |Fictional digital berde collection site|. We have molto |Kaliarda meaning 'a lot/many/much'| needs (px |Greek loan for 'e.g.'| the cost of UBI for the approx. 40 people we could take in in the next two months).

---

[2] I owe this word to Paola Revenioti and Panayiotis Evangelidis and the documentary Kaliarda (2015), directed by Paola Revenioti.

Please share through your contacts list and, as always, please get in touch with us to coordinate our efforts. Simply write us a brief text to introduce yourselves in any way you feel comfortable (name, pronouns, types of skills/ideas/support you could offer, and if you'd like please inform us of your neuropreferences so we can communicate with you in a way that feels good and works) and we promise to get back to you asap.

Warmly,
The Hospitality and Culture Working Group
Vangelija, Yassmine, Lamia, Ksenia, Gašo, Enar, Dulcinea, Ciwan, Casho, Bura, Abidemi, Åsa

Email from hcwg2@tutanota.com to all residents. 2.8.2037, 10:31

Taking flight from the concept of hospitality – lit. 'friendliness to guests' – important to many cultures in the basin, I want to share some thoughts on solidarity. People crossing land and sea under extremely precarious circumstances to ask for asylum under international law faced pushbacks, jail (upon accusations of smuggling), and/or deportations, all results of a very broad EU framework of criminalisation of facilitation of unauthorised entry. Volunteers working in sea rescue (captains and crew out at sea, administrators, lawyers, healthcare professionals on land and coordinators over the phone) relied on donations. Especially in the early 2020s with the rise of neofascism and the trials of asylum seekers accused of smuggling, like the #FreePylos9 or Homayoun Sabetara, the concept of hospitality – filoxenia – became ever more important in the South as the Centre implemented nativist fortress-focused policies. Many were fighting against borders, boundaries, binaries.

It's a region that is simultaneously my safe place and a site of immediate impact of environmental and geopolitical changes, a horrifying and treacherous place, a seametery.[3] *A site where both a fantasy and a nightmare can be (and currently are) situated and an array of sociopolitical, aesthetic and linguistic issues can be taken up. Water levels rising, a crumbling marine ecosystem, little to no rain, a rocky terrain with little soil, war, murders (colloquially referred to as 'pushbacks'), potential mineral resources in its various (often disputed) EEZs, fires, corruption, discrimination, violence, tourists and ερ μπι εν μπι. In between Asiaeurope, and Africa is the home to many traditionally poor communities, countries and areas, many*

[3] '"Mediterranean seametery", a neologism meant to capture the oxymoronic nature of the sea in which liquidity has become synonymous with immobility precipitated by preposterous and rigid policies that have transformed a sea into a cemetery' (Abderrezak 2021, 372–91).

having been part of the Ottoman Empire or other colonial and neocolonial regimes – a region that contains countries currently called Morocco, Algeria, Tunisia, Libya, Egypt, Palestine, Israel, Lebanon, Cyprus, Syria, Turkey, Greece, Albania, Montenegro, Bosnia and Herzegovina, Croatia, Slovenia, Italy, Malta, France, Monaco, Spain.

As Matvejević writes:

> *the Mediterranean is not merely geography. Its boundaries are drawn in neither space nor time. There is in fact no way of drawing them: they are neither ethnic nor historical, state nor national; they are like a chalk circle that is constantly traced and erased, that the winds and waves, that obligations and inspirations expand or reduce. The Mediterranean shores have seen not only the silk route but also the crisscrossing of many others: routes of salt and spices, amber and ornaments, oils and perfumes, tools and arms, skills and knowledge, arts and sciences. (Matvejević and Heim 1999, 9–10)*

It's a region spreading in and around water with a long history of exchange, cultural creations (beyond the Greco-Roman antiquity that so many narratives exclusively focus on), and resistance towards colonial regimes and exploitative industries.[4]

So far this sounds like a faux bubble of magical resistance in what reads like a textbook dystopian setting. Which is where social justice is relevant, I suppose. But maybe that's also all I can do right now. I can't escape my own anxieties. Even in order to create an escapist imaginary world, I rely on them. I don't know how else to think of social justice. This intellectual guessing game, creating characters, giving them characteristics, backstories, preferences, abilities and styles of speaking/writing, is what I've found as a way to cope. Ενιγουει, this should give me the space to also think and share ideas on solidarity. And of course explore (perhaps

[4] Khuri-Makdisi posits that: 'radicals and militants in these global, yet "(semi-)peripheral cities" [referring specifically to Cairo, Alexandria and Beirut] were transmitting information about international issues, discussing them on the pages of periodicals, on stage, or in public gatherings and hence appropriating them and participating in them. By doing so they were full participants in the making of a globalized world, albeit perhaps offering an alternative vision of this world or even challenging and subverting the version created and maintained by European imperialism. Radicals formed networks that were connected informationally, politically and organizationally, to international and internationalist movements and organizations that sought to promote leftist ideas and implement radical projects in various corners of the world' (Khuri-Makdisi 2010, 2, 17) and further down he clarifies that he is not simply interpreting this as a reactive movement.

'Certainly in Eastern Mediterranean cities workers actively shaped the language, media, and spaces of contestation and the culture of radicalism that spread in these cities, in the theater and songs, in coffeehouses, in the workplace, and on the streets workers in various sectors promoted a plethora of radical ideas' (Khuri-Makdisi 2010, 197).

cryptically at times) a queer (or whatever it may be called or not in the future) Med ethos of the future. One based on support systems and prioritising help, rest and disability. It could also open up a space to envision some form of accountability for invasions, occupations and exploitation. And I don't mean just buying a cezve or a ابريق during one's vacation by the sea or buying and renovating property and further driving up prices making it impossible for locals to find affordable housing ...

*It would be ideal to show not only creative writing on themes of social justice but also a paradigmatic shift towards the legitimisation of emotion and pleasure in public and formal discourse. Maybe even *gasps* in AcAdEMia!*

Natasha tells me of Beth Kamunge's thoughts, documented in The Fire Now: Anti-racist scholarship in times of explicit racial violence, *which question writing and ponder whether there is room for messy writing, that poses questions rather than answers them and embodies grief (Johnson 2018, 190). It's so difficult to write about worlds on fire and open up about one's grief and find pleasures and joys, especially in a short text where tilting from one to the other can seem so sudden and clunky.* ~~*I still don't*~~

The Origins

The beginning of the pandemic brought an inflow of emails and several new members/residents. I had joined a few months earlier. The project ran for several years, on a small scale, but the flight towards nature, small communities and the prospect of self-sustainability brought it to peoples' attention in the second half of 2020, with the emergence of the nationwide lockdowns. I still remember the shift in our workload, the social media tags and DMs, and the many, many conversations that followed. Our younger residents don't know a world where these projects were not the norm. Ours was premised on queer-feminist, egalitarian, anti-racist, anti-speciesist ideas.

I'm writing mainly in English because we speak mainly in English. Here and there my text will be interspersed with other languages, my first one, as well as words I learnt from friends, colleagues and fellow community members. I decided to write this account of my experiences in the community to reflect in particular on the changes that took place in the early post-COVID-19 years. 'Post-COVID-19', of course, means after it appeared.

I, myself, joined the collective in 2019, having visited some of their events with local friends while vacationing on the island in years prior. I was living in L at the time, having moved there from A to study. I was getting frustrated with the busy lifestyle and the size of the city and, to be honest, I was very unhappy with my studies. I worked at a café in I at the time. I was thinking of moving to a sunnier place for at least part of the year. I had befriended some of the islanders, who told me about the collective and, while I wasn't certain this was for me, I secretly entertained the idea of joining on a trial basis.

When I first started living here we were only about 40 people, some of whom lived here part-time. The farm and the stables didn't exist yet, we only had a fenced-off lot with two rescued goats. They got the project going in 2019 and I was happy to help with something hands-on. It was exactly the change I had been craving. I worked as a language teacher, over this first winter, in a small language school in the city centre. The children were very curious about me, but also prone to be mischievous, due to my not understanding them, but over time we were able to communicate more and more and we got along just fine. By the end of my first year, I felt like I had become part of the community. I realised I was a bit of a satellite to the local community of migrants and eXPaTs but was looking for something a little more layered and from my background. The collective taught me a lot and most people were very patient and generous, though we did have some tensions over how differently we understood expressions of racism, microaggressions and queerphobia and how we each preferred to deal with them in public. It was comforting to me that we were all antikarniotides |Neologism meaning 'vegetarian/ vegan'|, and I was elated to work at building the shelter and stables for all the rescues. You wouldn't believe what the rescues had been through …

Like the extrovert I am, I soon took up the role of forming the 'welcoming committee' for newcomers, something I still enjoy participating in. It has been great, drawing on my own experience, to inform people who are just joining about practical matters, as well as encourage the more reserved to join interest groups in order to acclimate and get comfy. I did feel like a counsellor during freshers' week, which was fun. It also allowed me to

I was also doing some graphic design and animation work, on the side, for online platforms and news sites. When I could support myself solely from graphic projects, I quit the language school. This meant I didn't have to go to the city daily and in the winter I barely went at all, which, combined with the fact that I was starting to miss going out on proper dates, made me feel somewhat isolated. That's when Bridget joined the collective and we hit it off right from the start. She was just so delightful and fun to be around and easy to talk to. ~~Soon we were a~~

~~couple and I felt at home. Showing her around was also a nice way for me to go out more and appreciate the beauty of the place once again. Soon, Bridget, her partner Sara, and I were a throuple and I felt at home. Showing them around was also a nice way for me to go out more and appreciate the beauty of the island once again.~~ Soon we were together and I felt at home. Showing her and others around was also a nice way for me to go out more and appreciate the beauty of nature here.

In the years that followed we would receive DMs and emails from time to time (especially during the end of the winter) and we would collectively discuss each person and have them over for a conversation (usually over dinner), or over Skype if they couldn't be here in person. The latter was always a struggle, as we prefer the more unstructured and organic way of a dinner to get to know someone and for them to get to know us and see first hand how the place functions. We would often get very different impressions when the meeting was exclusively online and went back and forth on our decision to offer this as a way to get to know a person.

There were, of course, situations where a meeting was unnecessary and would have been indeed unthinkable, such as the case of people fleeing from war (the ones already developing and those that broke out). Of course I joined before the big pandemics and the multi-war era. At that time seceding would have seemed a wild idea, to even think of, let alone propose and organise for an entire archipelago for decades, but that was then.

We began a crowdfunding campaign to get two caravans, as it was urgent to host three individuals (two of them underage) immediately and we hoped to then be able to raise the funds to build a few more lodgings. The campaign for the used caravans was successful, thanks to friends and contacts from all over, who shared and backed it. The berde for building, though, was much more difficult to gather, even with the lower costs, thanks to the collective doing some of the labour.

The next three years went on without major changes, I was still happily seeing Bridget, doing freelance design work and helping out, here and there, with hands-on tasks. My mom came for a visit in 2019. She said she could imagine retiring in such a 'commune'! As if!

I wasn't part of the pedagogy working group but I could see they were doing much-needed things. They embraced, and tried to implement, deinstitutionalised pedagogical processes, which included rocking chairs, group assignments, school supplies and clothes for all, full meals for all. Textbooks with drawings and pictures with different people and children, terminology that doesn't exclude, that speaks of Roma history, trans cultures, working classness, non-normative persons, children who grew up in the province, intersex children, deaf children who don't or can't have access to the services they need, children who are girls, children who have experienced violence, children who raised themselves.

Then, 2020 came round and things started changing drastically. In late February the country saw its first COVID-19 cases and by early March it went into a lockdown. This didn't affect those of us working from home or in the community, so much, but it was disastrous for those who worked in the service industry. For instance Ioanna's jewellery store had to close for more than two months and I helped her create her Etsy store and website. Ersi wasn't allowed to make the at-home visits to the elderly, so she too was unemployed. The salon, where Lena worked, closed, Sophia was asked to only clean the bank branch once a week, after the employees were off. Dina was an essential worker (working for the power company) and had to continue going to work. Laleh continued to work at the hospital, but she wasn't allowed to do house visits, and Lisa and Georgia continued working on the bikes and their sales slightly went up, as people were trying to find physically distant ways to commute and exercise. The government offered meagre benefits, for those financially impacted, that helped only a little and the campaigns for more lodgings and caravans were put on hold, as the whole world froze – and giving money to charity when you don't know if your next paycheck is coming in was, of course, too risky for many. I was lucky to have my services requested for those small businesses that wanted to transition to online platforms and I was able to provide for those of us that could not. After things calmed down, we would begin the long discussion and implementation of the UBI.

During this time, we turned to the garden project and the shelter, for comfort, to take our minds off things and to feel connected and active, though we were all somewhat numb. Summer came and most went back to work, some hoping tourism would cover some of the damages. It soon became clear that travel restrictions, financial concerns and people's fear over COVID-19 wouldn't allow us to go back to normal any time soon. It was a strenuous year that brought a depressive mood in the group and put several potential new members on hold.

Written by T. S. on January 23rd, 2040.

Lamia, a mixed-media artist and educator, joined the collective early on. This is her narration, written many years ago for a collective exhibition project. It looks back on the time she moved t/here | note: the stylisation is meant to indicate a position that may or may not be here or there |

Community Vacation

Not strictly prioritising joy and pleasure, but along lines of creating community structures to keep the life-work balance in check, my friend ~~ElenaRubaForozan~~ Elena, who works as a skipper and conservationist, added the following post on our community bulletin board.

> Ya flx,
>
> Several of us realised that we have been working hard the past two weeks with the preparations and all and our emotional lives, rest, and housework have suffered as a result. No doğru person |a person with a past, present, or future of what some of us today call illness, neuroatypicality, and/or disability| could do that. We are proposing to take the next three days off from our day jobs and hold them as community rest days, so we can catch up with each other, do chores, neurocover |neuro + recover|, and rest.
>
> How do you feel about that?
>
> Love,
>
> Elena
>
> *Sent on | the community's own developed encrypted messaging app | by Elena Ortega on March 17th, 2051*

It must have become more and more important for those who had grown up in South/Eastern Europe, the Balkans, the Near East, Middle East, North Africa, the (semi)Periphery, to work on shedding our/their shame for resting and help each other reflect on our/their hustling habits. When Northerners started discussing burnout and providing structures to keep it at bay (by working just under the threshold of melting down) we/they continued to work hard and work long days (and entire 'saisons') |that refers to the May to October jobs with no days off catering to the whims of tourists| often without childcare provisions, overtime compensations, or full insurance and pension benefits. Some of them were forced to sign papers declaring worksite accidents (fall in the shipyard, traffic accidents with a delivery motorbike, traffic accident on the way to work) as 'domestic' ones so the company wouldn't have to pay. In the collective they tried to be there for one another and aimed at reducing the amount of work hours focusing on restoring their bodies and relationships, resting and doing absolutely nothing, but also, for those who want to, continuing education, developing hobbies and doing care work. The struggle of overcoming the stereotype of the lazy ___________, the slow _________, the endless siesta-haver, and being open about the way they/we chose to work, doesn't stop. They shared resources in order to be able to afford better lives.

It's difficult to find joys and pleasures at the /sʌɪt/[5] *of constant mournings. Femicides, Helin Bölek, Zackie Oh!, Марѝца, Lesbos, Fuerteventura, and and and … According to Derrida, friendship (φιλία) begins with the possibility of survival (2020, 14) and surviving is the grieved act of loving (2020, 14). Friendship is what kicked this whole project off and what maintained it. Friendships and loves of the unmournable.*

Athanasiou, focusing on the politics of agonistic mourning in the case of Žene u Crnom (Women in Black), examines the grievability strategies of feminists 'who enact grief and memory despite and against the biopolitics of warfare and its concomitant interpellating lines of heteronormative bloodline kinship and militarist national sovereignty' (2017, 12–13). The collective have been compiling such an archive of the lives of unmournables with the intention to send it to us and perhaps people in other temporalities.

Maybe that is what the fragment of this embroidery I found is, too …

[5] IPA and stand-in for both site and sight.

Break for a positive activity: listening to a στ_οργισμένο song, like this one: https://tinyurl.com/LySeBi.

Sex Party

13.05.2064, 10:37 A: Do we address them directly?

13.05.2064, 10:39 K: @A That's what the consensus at the workshop was last weekend. And adding sx~. I think it should be more informal and dirtier

13.05.2064, 11:04 E: @K Wanna add some of the dirtier elements? I thoughts of 'ελάτε να μοντερνιστούμε' but not sure this is what you meant.

13.05.2064, 11:05 R: I have to say I really hate the name (>⌒<). Can we go back to something less … iconic?

13.05.2064, 11:05 S: @A adding götveren and maricas this time for one!

13.05.2064, 13:11 K: Tahrijah and Ruba from AWA confirmed they will be there and will arrange for two more people to join for the remaining shifts on top of the sexual assistants and the interpreters.

13.05.2064, 14:23 R: @K This is brilliant! Thank you <3

14.05.2064, 20:31 B: Cipriano, Pet ve Loki önümüzdeki toplantımıza katılmaktan mutluluk duyacaklarını söyledi.

15.05.2064, 14:28 R: @B <3 I adapted the second paragrafı[6] and added the elements we talked about yesterday. It now looks like that: 'Both nights are organised by teams that include locals and guests, as well as sex professionals (workers, educators, certified assistants) and intend to be inclusive* and accessible* spaces of fun and connection. Feel free to bring your own assistant along, but please inform us on registration. You are welcome to drop by and stay for as long as you like whichever time of day or night.'

15.05.2064, 14:52 E: @B Thank you for taking care of that. Btw I think we should add something about the intensity like 'Some times are usually quieter (12pm–5pm) whereas others are usually more busy (8pm–3am).' Also maybe the 'intend to be inclusive* and accessible*' sounds too retro?

15.05.2064, 15:05 M: and the erotica

15.05.2064, 15:05 S: @M Yes, I'll send it to you asap to send it to those who opt in in the form.

[6] Turkish word.

15.05.2064, 15:06 M: @S Thank you!

16.05.2064, 04:03 K: I need ‘dezontupu’ to be part of it re ˘ف˘

16.05.2064, 12:19 M: @K @S I added götveren, maricas, and dezontupudes. Check if you agree with addition.

17.05.2064, 09:33 S: I just received the supplies. Will check the invitation text before it goes out today. Any last minute wishes anyone?

17.05.2064, 09:54 M: @S Looks great, thank you insancıklar mou!

17.05.2064, 10:02 E: Thank you everyone, looks good!

17.05.2064, 10:43 K: Looks ready to go, to me! You all smashed it!

Group chat on ◌ between M4ria, S., Elya, Katerina, Rabia, B3 and Adalia, the Pleasure Principles

The politics of resistance and survival require experimenting with new styles, forms and methods, to undo the calcification of canons and instead play with each other and with all materials available to us (crucially language). Fragmented Med sci-fi, messaging app texts, unfinished thoughts based on unfinished readings, new old lore, unfinished embroidery, all have their place here.

References

Abderrezak, Hakim. 2016. *Ex-Centric Migrations: Europe and the Maghreb in Mediterranean cinema, literature, and music*. Bloomington: Indiana University Press.

Abderrezak, Hakim. 2021. 'The Mediterranean sieve, spring and seametery'. In *Refugee Imaginaries: Research across the humanities*, edited by Emma Cox, Sam Durrant, David Farrier, Lyndsey Stonebridge and Agnes Woolley, 372–91. Edinburgh: Edinburgh University Press.

Al Numan, Yiannis. 2032. *Syrian-Greek Assemblages*. Rodos: Turan.

Althusser, Louis. 2016. *Lenin and Philosophy and Other Essays*. n.p.: Aakar Books.

Athanasiou, Athena. 2017. *Agonistic Mourning: Political dissidence and the Women in Black*. Edinburgh: Edinburgh University Press.

B. Jones, Niesha. 2034. *Fat & Fierce Femininities*. Antwerp: Coutinho.

Blagojević, Marina. 2009. *Knowledge Production at the Semiperiphery: A gender perspective*. Belgrade: Institut za kriminološka i sociološka istraživanja.

Derrida, Jacques. 2020. *The Politics of Friendship*. London: Verso.

Fagunwa, Oluwafunbi. n.d. 'Navigating coastal healing: A roadmap to understanding and implementation', *The Tramuntanatlantic*.

Glissant, Édouard, translated by Betsy Wing. 1997. *Poetics of Relation*. Ann Arbor: University of Michigan Press.

Johnson, Azeezat, Remi Joseph-Salisbury and Beth Kamunge (eds). 2018. *The Fire Now: Anti-racist scholarship in times of explicit racial violence*. London: Zed Books.

Khuri-Makdisi, Ilham. 2010. *The Eastern Mediterranean and the Making of Global Radicalism, 1860–1914*. Berkeley: University of California Press.

Koobak, Redi, Madina Tlostanova and Suruchi Thapar-Björkert (eds). 2021. *Postcolonial and Postsocialist Dialogues: Intersections, opacities, challenges in feminist theorizing and practice*. New York : Routledge. https://doi.org/10.4324/9781003003199.

Matvejević, Predrag and Michael Henry Heim. 1999. *Mediterranean: A cultural landscape*. Berkeley: University of California Press.

Mayerchyk, Maria and Olga Plakhotnik. 2021. 'Uneventful feminist protest in post-maidan Ukraine: nation and colonialism revisited'. In *Postcolonial and Postsocialist Dialogues: Intersections, opacities, challenges in feminist theorizing and practice*, edited by Redi Koobak, M. V. Tlostanova and Suruchi Thapar-Björkert, 121–37. New York: Routledge.

Mazē, Maria. 2023. *Klōtsies Me Dōdekaponta: Hē Analysē Henos Syllogikou Emeis Meta Tē Dolophonia Tou Zak/Tēs Zaki*. Thessalonikē: Ekdoseis Psēphides.

Mbembe, Achille and Steve Corcoran. 2019. *Necropolitics*. Durham, NC: Duke University Press.

Muñoz, José Esteban. 2009. *Cruising Utopia: The then and there of queer futurity*. New York: New York University Press.

Rebane, Edenema. 2060. 'A premiere focusing on DIY film-making and an after-party full of accessible pleasures', *The Conversationalist*, 25 May.

Rostami, Rekan. 2062. 'Redefining the boundaries of bodies through quantum physics', *Physikis Analysis* 6(2): 245–53.

Schmidt, Rolf. 2059. 'Deutschland ruft diplomaten aus Astana Zurück, weil es gegen "Ausländische agenten" vorgehen will', *Der Berliner Klugscheisser*.

Smith, Jolene. 2060. 'NUS further becoming a capitalist monopoly monarchy', *The Insider*, 3 December.

Stojanovska, Petka. 2063. 'Counselling those who want to rehabilitate: Challenges and realistic goals', *010* 3, no. Digital Rehabilitation.

T., Anna. 2020. 'Opacity-minority-improvisation: An exploration of the closet through queer slangs and postcolonial theory', *Queer Studies* 27. Bielefeld: Transcript.

Western, Tom. 2021. 'Notes on an anticolonial Athens', *Decolonize Hella* blog, 3 August. Accessed 28 July 2025. https://decolonizehellas.org/en/notes-on-an-anticolonial-athens/.

Xanim, Zerya. 2060. 'Fighting with empathy and generosity: learning from non-human animals'. In *Session 1: Liberation for All*. Peras.

Πετρόπουλος, Γιώργος. 2023. 'Το Πένθος Ως Queer Μεθοδολογία: Ο Ζακ Ντεριντά Συνομιλεί Με Την Τζούντιθ Μπάτλερ', *Feministiqa* 6 Winter. Accessed 9 October 2025. https://feministiqa.net/to-penthos-os-queer-methodologia/.

This project is one that required research in disciplines and fields I have merely superficial/passing knowledge in/of. The creative part was like structuring a performance or an installation, it was about dramaturgy, symbols, my role, the interaction with you. The emotionally challenging part was trying to talk about all these without losing hope. Thinking of the environment, the societies and their societies and their communities and their people and their people and their communities and their societies and their societies and their environment was the pleasurable part. ~~It's rare to have so much creative writing freedom and~~ I'm very thankful to have been included in this project.

*These documents were chosen to give you an idea of the themes and discourse. They present Is and wes, and share thoughts and feelings from members of the collective. Some of the documents have been published in the book Δiotima; or, Δeir*land: A fragmented stori of arkivs, kolektivism, imaginaʃon, & multituds (FAC, 2025).*

They are meant to give you an idea of what life in the collective, in that society, in that there and then is/was/will be like. They are interspersed with hints to the linguistic backgrounds, the linguistic adaptation itself being such a synthetic process (combining regional languages with minority slangs, reclaiming terms, indicating and resisting against asymmetrical influences from without).

I hope you enjoyed joining this text-performance. I enjoyed working on it and will continue to do so. You are welcome to get in touch to discuss the issues and/or artistic/creative choices made in this experimental text. Perhaps you'd like to share your own work, maybe we can collaborate in a future (or past) project. Thank you for being here.

Warmly,
A.

7
The interview: scholarship, sincerity, suspicion

Dilar Dirik

In memory of Nagihan and Gulan

Clarity is key to academic knowledge production, which – at least in theory – derives its strength from its ability to make sense of complex, connected phenomena through objectivity, nuance and critique. While the merits of this approach are widely known, scholarly representations of real-life situations are necessarily limited by conventional epistemic forms – hegemonic inside academia – and the material conditions that organise knowledge under capitalism in a nation-statist world system.

Since 2014, the year in which Kurdistan entered mass global consciousness due to the massacres of and the resistance against the so-called Islamic State, Kurdish people, women in particular, have interacted with thousands of people from around the world, who came into their lives with countless questions and agendas. In this period, marked by intensive periods of war, military operations, occupation campaigns, forced displacement, mass incarceration and numerous assassinations in Kurdistan, many people with links to foreign governments, political parties, intelligence services and embassies, presented themselves as independent researchers, who had come to produce objective, 'policy-relevant' knowledge on the newly-discovered Kurds. One major dynamic shaping the interaction between researchers and interlocutors is the terror-labelling of the Kurdistan Workers' Party (PKK) not only by regional countries, but by powerful geopolitical actors such as the US, the EU and individual European countries.

Over the period of a decade, I tried to navigate this complex terrain, as a young researcher, volunteer amateur translator and organiser. One of the most insight-offering aspects of my experience has been the chance to observe how the ways in which different people and groups, due to their political and geopolitical positioning in the world system, inhabit different epistemic worlds, and how this often makes their references for truth and reality nearly irreconcilable with those of others. Growing up around the spiritually and politically rich cosmology of the Kurdistan Freedom Movement and seeing the ways in which it came to be represented in emerging scholarly accounts, I have long been intrigued by the lack of reflection even among critical scholars on their ideological positionality, especially in the context of interview settings and ethnographic accounts. Having myself been in different positions of various interview settings (researcher, interviewee or translator), and as someone who produces knowledge in a politically engaged way (now outside of academia), I at times found behavioural dynamics around interviews more revealing than the verbal exchanges constructed as their content. Dynamics are often further inflamed in a context of violence and repression.

In interviews, activists in the Kurdish women's liberation movement usually not only talk about their lives when engaging with outsiders, but, in line with ideological-political cultures and convictions, also systematically relay entire worldviews and values that inform the way they move and act in the world. To some researchers, however, as I gleaned from conversations with interviewees and my own observations in the field and in the literature, the believability of Kurdish women's self-making narratives hinges upon a liberal, secular sense of coherence. A certain lack of understanding or patience towards oppressed and struggling people's freedom dreams, coupled with overstatements of the implications of one's findings, can result in a failure among researchers to read the affective meanings attributed to people, causes and ideals. For example, from the perspective of Kurdish revolutionaries, activists and ordinary people, who were largely invisible in literature until 2014, it is often seen as a duty to perform one's people's pride, to do justice to repressed histories and to remember martyrs. Mantra-like repetitions of political lines, believed in, embodied and died for, are cultural world-making tools. Researchers who embark on research quests with the frequently stated objective of wanting to explore gaps between 'romanticised' discourse and 'objective' reality, fail to realise that spoken words must not necessarily be interpreted as definite statements on already achieved situations, but rather as optimistically expressing a sense of duty to fight for political possibilities, the outcomes of which depend on collective struggle. Given the high rates of martyrdom in Kurdistan, speech acts of revolutionaries are also a form of self-making and memorialisation. The interview is an opportunity to archive and immortalise one's individual self by speaking one's lived or imagined meanings into recorded history. These ritualistic remembrances, in turn, have frequently been dismissed as superficial, performative 'official lines', by feminist researchers, who, for their own purposes, were keen on capturing complexity and vulnerability. Their curiosity or insistence on pursuing certain lines of interrogation (such as individual stories to describe agency, with effort to identify instances of tension, contradiction and failure to signal a 'critical lens') can be met with impatience by their interlocutors. While scepticism is a key tool of academic critique, it is not always a mindset that political movements, especially those with revolutionary utopias and mass appeal, can afford. Or rather, the respective objects of critique can diverge greatly. Beyond the immediate material political context marked by asymmetric power relations, interactions between researchers and interlocutors often also express different senses or concerns around security, morality, historiographic responsibility, temporality, audience, cosmology, epistemic and linguistic affect and awareness of social complexities.

Meanwhile, another common curatorial practice among researchers, journalists and translators is to – seemingly for a higher purpose – boost and further embellish with meaning and depth, claims, sometimes questionable ones, nonchalantly uttered by their interlocutors, especially if these are in one way or another in positions of relative vulnerability. While care, feelings of solidarity and empathy, a sense of justice or belief in change may drive them, such tendencies also often display projection, that is, ways of validating researchers' own undeclared desires and dreams. What safer way to communicate one's politics, within the framework of liberal universities nonetheless, than indirectly, through the stories of others, in grant-generating papers? Of course, the oppressed and the resisting, too, sometimes deceive, exaggerate, misrepresent or manipulate. They sometimes feel they must. Accounts and narratives can shape the course of events, especially in the current age of communication.

These and other questions become even more morally urgent in contexts marked by violence and loss. What are the ethics of making framing statements about people who are in struggle during an interview and die for their ideals soon after? In what ways does the increasing adherence of higher education institutions to neoliberal market demands impact researchers' ability to produce intellectual labour with historical, political and philosophical depth and awareness?

The following is an experiment in conveying suppressed (inter) personal and political sentiments and dynamics in interview settings that undoubtedly exist (alongside geopolitical realities), but are, for various reasons, including professional etiquette, considered inappropriate to acknowledge: poor communication, tension, vanity, anxiety, pettiness, jealousy, arrogance, deceit, boredom, manipulation and calculation, among others. It is a satirical critique based on personal experience as well as conversations with research interlocutors, activists, researchers and translators. The scenario constructed here is fictional, but the dynamics represented reflect a caricature appreciable by those familiar with the context of research around Kurdistan in the past decade.

My argument is implicitly conveyed and relates to epistemology. I take the liberty to communicate, albeit theatrically, things that *I just feel that I know*. This means that while I did not systematically, scientifically, methodically study the dynamics I problematise, I hold that, at the very least, I should be free to be honest about believing that sometimes some insights are simply true, and that I know that I know certain things just because I know. In most moments in life, human beings behave in society based on such cognition. Below, the dramatised parts of the chapter challenge what I see as a categoric (though often selective) hostility within academic scholarship towards people's intuition. Stemming from things like political sensitivity and emotional intelligence, intuitive knowledge develops not sporadically through 'the literature' but cumulatively in life. As an epistemic source, embodied knowledge is frequently fetishised in gender and race studies, but rarely taken seriously when it is a classed meaning-making position or diverts from the ideological liberalism prevalent within academia. Conventional approaches to research can furthermore rob researchers of the ability to note or value the mysteries of the universe – in this case, for example, the psychic connections that can develop between travellers on the same path, or the prophetic dreams and visions that feel very real to people, who often also act on them. It castrates imagination and knowledge of the human experience. During my PhD fieldwork and subsequently, during my write-up, I, too, had enigmatic encounters that I did not write about, as they neither had meaningful space within accepted scholarly conventions nor within their critiques. I suppressed entire spiritual worlds, truths, inside of me, in the effort to be taken seriously as a scholar in what is essentially a dogmatically secular field of operations, meant for a minority gaze.

Throughout, to challenge the vanity within ideas around scholarly rigour and individual authorship, I deliberately confuse the reader by blurring the lines between the self and the other, academia and life, reality and drama, to recreate a sense of emotional and intellectual chaos that often accompanies research and writing. Various aspects of this chapter are also humorous and self-critical takes on tendencies within feminist (and other) forms of qualitative knowledge outputs that draw on various methodological tools and engage in word acrobatics to communicate researchers' own agendas, desires and frustrations in apolitical, yet seemingly scholarly ways, to the often extremely small number of people who can access academic publications and the even smaller groups that bother to read the work.

***

The interview is about to begin. The phones are going to be put in the other room. The researcher is visibly irritated. Her ethnographic method will be compromised.

I need to use my phone to record the conversation.

> *You don't have a recording device? You can use mine, no problem. But we can't have phones here.*

Why? Isn't that a bit … extreme? I'd like to move around freely to get a sense of your lives.

> *This is part of the security measures here; I thought you knew that. Also, can you please not take photos here? I'll let you know when and where you can.*

Does everyone here have to obey such rules?

> *She seems unhappy about the measures.*
>
> > *Every day, another liability! What are we bringing upon ourselves …*
>
> *Look, let's try to make her comfortable, you know how they represent these things to the outside – coercion, paranoia …*
>
> > *Ouf, these people truly don't know a thing about the real world. Maybe she would join our class on surveillance? What do you think?*
>
> *Do you want me to translate that?*

And so, the interview starts.

On a scale from one to ten, how do you rate … ?

> > *We don't subscribe to positivist knowledge paradigms that quantify and measure life along …*

The interviewee elaborates at length on their collective critiques of the hegemonic forms of social science. Unimpressed, the researcher writes down a single sentence. Anyway, as a qualitative researcher, she did not like such questions either, but she had been told that quantitative papers were more likely to attract funding and publication. The first half hour passes in similar fashion. It is within the profession of both researchers and revolutionaries, the art of not exhibiting one's boredom.

A sensitive question is posed. The response needs to strike a balance between politics and truth. Too much or too little of either will create either geopolitical risk or spiritual harm.

The translator raises her eyebrows. The interviewee raises hers back. They telepathise for a few moments.

> *Please don't mess this up. We worked hard to get you this sort of attention.*
>
> *What do you want me to do? Lie? Bluff? Why are we doing this?*
>
> *You don't understand how these people think, but I do. I know what you want to say but you can't say that, it will backfire.*
>
> *What am I supposed to do then? Talk about the weather?*
>
> *Don't make our other efforts fall apart with your dogmatism in one instance. Speak in their language to get empathy. Don't you remember what happened after the last reporter?*
>
> *I want empathy for my truth. Our martyrs did not die for us to write a soap opera version of our struggle! Translate everything exactly as I say.*

As the two women, who will appear in the outputs as author and interlocutor respectively, lean back in their seats with a sense of ennui, a pendulum swings back and forth between them. This is the translator, whose body mobilises into awkward shapes in the quest to facilitate this encounter. A politically-engaged person herself, diasporic, she struggles to do justice to both worlds. Her blood pressure rises as the interviewee depicts a life of harsh conditions. Her heart smiles as she hears stories of resistance. She grows pensive as the researcher asks questions. Her critical faculties get stimulated, she visualises new ideas with interest and excitement. Although her presence is passive and her labour invisible to the consumers of both the research output and the movement's outward appearance, this nameless volunteer, too, has a stake in the outcome of this interaction. As she carries the burden of weaving a bridge of understanding (and maybe even solidarity), she also holds power over communication and information. Her interpretations will, to some extent, define the course of history. By the end of the interview, her facial expressions will have covered a palette of human emotions. She is self-conscious and afraid that her complex inner rollercoaster will reflect as unreliability. Increasingly sorry for herself, the translator's face begins to grow tense, subliminally signalling a sense of exhaustion to the others. *Come on guys, you know what's going on. Help me out here.*

The other two observe the translator's ordeal. A staring contest begins. Who is going to benefit from this round of translation? Concentrating, each one tries to pick up words that they recognise from the other's language. The translator's eyes scan the room for cues, searching for higher epistemological guidance. Her word-summoning fingers look like those of a witch performing magic. A referee, on trial by suspicious parties, who clearly is trying her best. But it is not clear to anyone, herself included, whether she grapples with the language or with how to best present one's words to the other.

I want to talk about sexuality.

Ob-vious-ly.

See *what* she is after? The interviewee smirks at the translator, who briefly twitches her eyebrows. The researcher is intrigued. The telepathy session is interrupted by the scratching sound of her previously resting pen. The native eyebrow pairs relax and curve over two artificial smiles. The interviewee calmly communicates familiar lines in response to the anticipated question. Impatient with the bureaucratic tone, the researcher suddenly turns to the translator.

So, what about you? Why don't you have sex?[1]

I never said anything like that.

So, you do?

Why are you asking me *now?*

I'm an ethnographer. I ask everyone things, not just in interviews. You are here, too, no? So, you signed up for these ideas, too? Or are there tensions? … You don't need to translate this to her, I can interview you later if you are up for it.

The translator is provoked. For the sake of political-intellectual harmony, she had refrained from setting her boundaries, and this was the result. Do personal boundaries exist in ethnography anyway?

> *She is trying to outwit us with pseudo-intellectual manoeuvres. Just because she calls herself a researcher, does she get to penetrate all our personal space? I don't mind these topics in principle. But who is she that I should share my private life with her, and in front of these comrades I just met yesterday? What do I do now? I'm not prepared for an intimate*

---

[1] This question was actually posed to the author by a well-known Western feminist in a recorded public event.

conversation with a dodgy stranger, not today. But if I tell her off, she will go ahead and write about how suppressed we all are … No, no, I don't trust her at all. She gave me police vibes from the start. She'll get a diplomatic answer, that's it.

Instead of saying the above, the translator bursts into a nervous giggle, which the researcher unimaginatively interprets as response to the taboos imposed on her. Nicely, she now has four anecdotes to choose from to introduce her hypothesis on embodied trauma and whatnot.

At this stage, the researcher is confused. She had been given the impression that she would be able to ask all her questions without reservation. But there is evidently a script, a non-state official narrative, and no matter how much she contextualises it, with empathy even, it is one that she must either endorse or challenge. The individuals she interacts with are like shapeshifters; they regularly update their identities, statuses, roles and levels of involvement – heck, even their names! She is walking on hot coals. With all these socio-political codes and mannerisms she is expected to follow, she doesn't know anymore what to ask. There is something surreal about the situation. She has an almost erotic attraction to the worlds these women draw, but she knows she must protect herself from charms, to stay grounded in reality – in the reality that she knows and that her intended audience is anchored in.

She barely follows as the interlocutor takes a dive into the long history of patriarchy and the state, elaborating at length about the function of sexuality under capitalism.

Seriously, how am I supposed to make sense of these people? Some of them totally lack self-awareness. No way are they as coherent as they make it out to be. The men in my life back home fetishise them and the unrealistic standards they propagate, so that they can continue oppressing us. And then this passes as revolutionary femininity, and I am supposed to swallow everything they say or else I am a White liberal colonial feminist. Life is more complex than these make-believe worlds, and we should know this as feminists. I'm trying my best to write you into bodies of knowledge, and you are here acting like you are outside of history, an exception, an alien who doesn't have a sex drive like everyone else, as if that's a good thing. Give me a break!

She takes a leap.

I am not that interested in these collective narratives, you see. They are repetitive, and I can read them online. I want you to speak more honestly about your challenges. Surely, it's not all that wonderful.

> *Who said that things are easy or perfect? Nobody knows our contradictions better than we do, and we address these internally. It seems that you came here with an agenda to detect all our issues and prove something when we never claimed to be flawless.*

I'm not trying to catch anyone off guard. I'm just asking critical questions. This is what feminist research is about. If you value criticism and self-criticism, as you say you do, then you should appreciate my questions, no?

> *There is a fine line between research and intelligence gathering.*

Are you accusing me of something?

> *What do we know about you? How do we know what you will do with all this information? The West has a history of infiltrating and undermining movements through 'research'.*

You think that they send feminists on precarious university contracts to subvert political struggles? That's quite a stretch!

> *That doesn't matter. Intelligence services are always ahead of the curve. Basic special warfare. There are plenty of unwitting agents out there.*[2] *Many are not even aware of the agendas they are part of.*

This part of the conversation, of course, never happened. Instead, the researcher abandons her hopes of arresting the mystery she came here for. On a certain level, she feels hurt by the group's inability to bond as humans. She tried her best to be compassionate and respectful. Even if she was not going to get to write up everything she witnessed, at least she wanted to understand. And that, for some reason, is not possible. She did, however, wonder why her subconscious produced such a dialogue about her research. She seems to have cracked the code of the extreme and repetitive discourse she has been exposed to. Or maybe it's her funding source.

Meanwhile, the interviewee has flashbacks. Her palms are sweaty. Anxiety, growling in her bowels.

> *Run, rush, live as quickly as possible.*
> *Shots in Paris, drones in Kobanê, another assassination.*
> *What am I doing here? Who is this person in front of me? Why is she asking this?*
> *Have I revealed too much? Was I too reserved?*
> *Will I live to know what she says about me?*

[2] This is not an exaggeration for dramatic effect.

> *Every sentence must do justice to our martyrs. At our most perfect selves we honour their sacrifices.*
> *I'm very tired. In the communal struggle, there is no Room of One's Own.*

Soon, a mild sense of panic creeps in. For everyone involved, albeit for different reasons, it is essential to end on a friendly note. During tea break, conversations continue.

> *I don't know why we keep giving interviews. These people portray themselves as objective, free from influences. They come here to prove the supremacy of their ideologies and lifestyles, and they are not honest about it. I would take their scepticism seriously if I knew they paid attention to social struggles on their doorsteps. Even their best have minds colonised by liberalism. They see the world burning, and they know they must act, but they first need to prove that being radical is not the way to go, that revolution is utopia. That's what is happening. If it isn't their states that send them here, that is!*

I really don't think it's that deep. She is quite inexperienced; I think she was genuinely intrigued by all the media images and wants to understand what's happening here. Her writing is not too bad, quite empathetic actually. The kind of writing we used to dream of. Besides, she has a point about the contradictions … It's good to have external critical engagement.

> *Sure, but for that you need philosophical depth – so don't say that too much in front of her. And aren't the interviews enough? I'd rather not have her see everything. I mean, damn, we can't even offer tea when the male comrades visit without feeling observed and wondering how she will interpret every move.*

You see, in ethnography – I know this from my time at uni – they stress the role of the so-called 'everyday'. So even a coincidence or anecdote can become a powerful, meaningful metaphor if you pull it off in the right way. There is value in that, but it comes at the cost of material analysis. I know an anthropologist, who managed to stretch one ten-minute conversation with two people she just met into three book chapters.

> *I mean, we do value theorising from life, but not in this robotic fashion, without historical and political awareness of colonialism and power. No wonder they are so clueless about the real world. Anyway, make sure to get her contact details. Maybe she can help us with things in the future.*

The translator gives the researcher her phone back.

You would be a great research assistant. You know so much about the context, and you know how to engage westerners. You are different, you know. You have potential – if you know what I mean.

> *I'm actually involved in the work here, we do research, too, but our approach and perspectives are different from the dominant system. We try to …*

I know. Take my card anyway. I'm part of a decolonial feminisms research cluster. Think about it. Some critical distance will be good for you. You guys need to engage the world if you want recognition.

Tired, the translator quietly disappears, to go for a smoke. Meanwhile, the other two remember that they need to log this encounter for their own respective purposes.

Let's

take

a photo.

Loooong live the women's struggle!

Six months later, the interviewee dies in an airstrike. The researcher gets a permanent contract. The translator struggles with finances and mental health and remembers the card. And then the martyrs. And then, again, the card. Then the martyrs again.

***

This chapter is dedicated to two Kurdish revolutionaries, Gulan (Eylem Kaplan) and Zîlan (Nagihan Akarsel), whom I got to spend time with during my research. The perspectives – developed inside war, amid bombardments – that they shared with me on the need for liberationist knowledge production outside of mainstream institutions had a great impact on me. Gulan was killed in combat in 2016, a year after I interviewed her. Zîlan was assassinated in 2022, by an agent of the Turkish intelligence, in front of her home in Silêmanî, where she was building up what is now the Kurdish Women's Library, Archive and Research Center.

Part IV

Reparative rigour: caring for the archives of the living and the dead

8 Writing at the limits of reason: or, why is it so damn hard to write? We were never meant to be written; we were meant to dance

MJ Hunter Brueggemann, Bea Wohl and Koundinya Dhulipalla

Prelude

Following the main body of this chapter are two appendices: Appendix 2 presents two reworked versions of the same chapter text you are currently reading, while Appendix 1 explains how they were generated. The two supporting derivatives of this main text explore the form, process and methods of the text's production through obfuscation, re-expression, derivation and exploitation, using computational encryption with the tool duckyfuzz (Figure 8.1).

One encoded version uses temporality as a modality through which the central writing becomes encoded and transformed. The two texts are mutually interchangeable, but only at a specific moment in time. An instance that has evidently passed. The other version is encoded in a similar manner, but in this case, 'location' is the anchor by which the poetic re-expression maintains its relation to the source writing. Like the first, it converts the original text into a new form based on location data, resulting in text that diverges in readability. Both encoded texts lose their meaning in familiar languages yet continue to retain the translation in languages unknown. Both the time and space temporalities are ever changing, directly influencing this encoding process, bringing the author and authorship into the text, but emphasising the contextuality through which textuality is approached. This is achieved through the logic of computational systems, but it aims to yield nothing that seeks

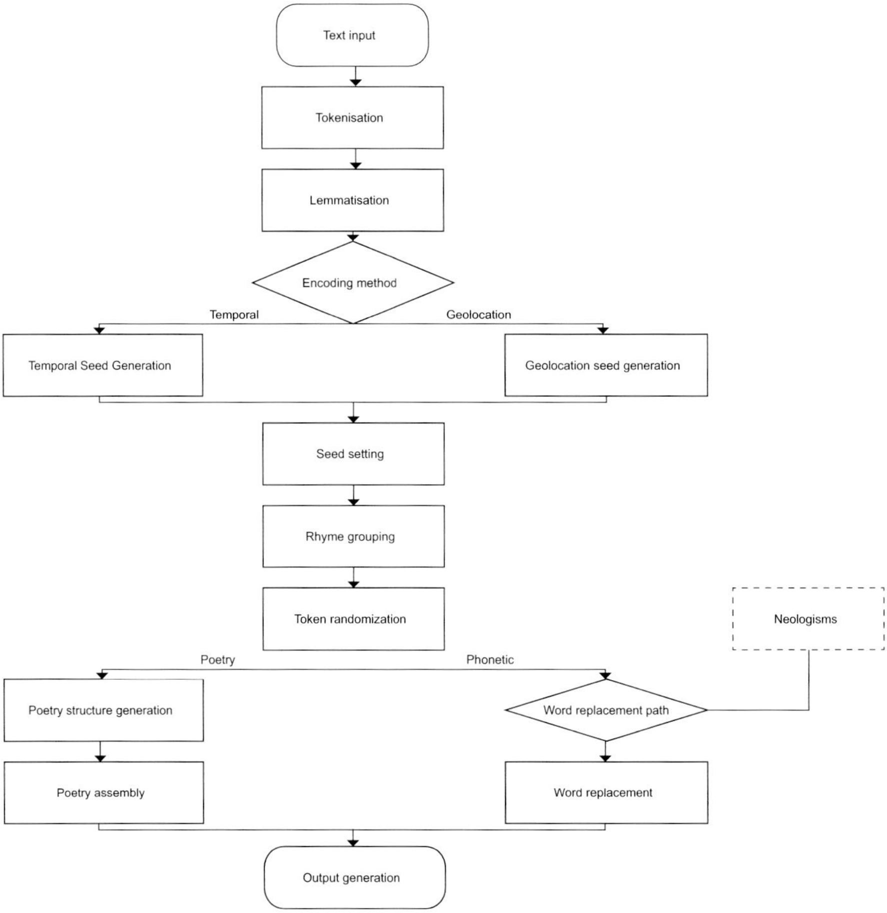

Figure 8.1 Workflow diagram for duckyfuzz. *Source*: © Koundinya Dhulipalla, 2025.

to be reasonable as such. It is a matter of celebrating the irrationality of context, an affirmation that draws attention to the singularity of marginality and, in turn, gestures toward the limits of reason, or more precisely, the emergence of other forms of reason.

Movement I

> Publishing standards tend to construct detached, 'objective', 'rational', inaccessible writing as good writing … Is there room for 'messy' writing that calls for speculation? that poses more questions than it does answers? that embodies grief and lament – a dirge of sorts? (Kamunge 2018, 190)

My dear former self,
My dear future students,
And those whom I did not get to know because you are unjustly missing,

We sought to solve the conundrum of the brutality of writing *for* you. While it remains unsolved, we hope our efforts are not wasted. If this only demonstrates how not to pursue this endeavour, my work will still have been useful.

We know *spoon theory* (the energy allocation metaphor, see Miserandino 2017), the social models of gender, race, sexuality, ageism, poverty, the theories concerning invisible labour and all-too-easily uttered calls for inclusive epistemologies of knowing. These methods come to mind when we think of the tools and supposed allies in creating inclusive epistemic sanctuaries within academia and the academic form. Calls on this matter are widespread and loud and hence we feel that responding to these encouragements ought to be easy (or at least welcomed). But it is this very ease, or the illusion of straightforwardness, we shall dwell on in this chapter.

Those who enjoy the privilege of feeling epistemologically at ease within the halls of academia may find it difficult, if not impossible, to comprehend what it means to be epistemically polyglot, to experience the visceral, embodied alienation of one's own mind by the need to express and inhabit ways of knowing that diverge from what feels affirming. This chapter, however, is a lament that emerges from within the ivory tower's walls. We assert that, regardless of our location, we unapologetically seek to maintain our voice, accents and *inflections of the margins* of home. In our work, we purposefully share experiences in an attempt to foster resistance, epistemological self-advocacy, and allyship for those poorly served by the status quo. We aim to offer a provocative challenge to the academic medium, not merely in theory but, emphatically, in practice.

Uncertainty is inherent to queer life, it is itself part of the queer experience, it is a queer practice. Queerness itself, by merely existing, challenges the erasure of uncertainty in academic practice; uncertainty and the unknown are positioned as opponents of firm knowing and knowledge. Our queerness, as an unstable category, becomes problematic and threatening due to its opposition to conventionality, and as we refuse to be split from our bodies, our queerness remains inseparable from us.

Disabled and mad individuals have long been objectified through the gaze of able-bodied onlookers, perceived as sources of 'awe, pity, wonder, amusement, scorn, disgust, and anxiety', thrust into the spotlight by a cultural pedagogy that emphasises difference in a fashion that more than anything alienates, not heals (Hogg 2020, 73). This experience is captured in the poignant reflection: 'I am highly visible but regularly treated as invisible' (Wolframe 2013, 208, in Hogg 2020, 74). This isn't just a paradox of existence; it challenges how we are treated, prompting the question: by whose logic are we judged so contradictorily?

'Our (Trans*) bodies are fragmented and internally contradictory' (Hogg 2020, 71), a reflection on identity that exposes the obsolescence of reason, shows us what it means to be 'writing at the limits of reason'. Marginalisation is experienced and it is produced. It is the outcome of a complex system of differing interfering processes. It puts into question how we know and account for our knowing. See who this way of knowing serves? Whose way of knowing gets maintained through it, and whose utterances are judged unstable right from the outset? The pluriversality of marginalisation is, by design, intended to enforce submission. In the realm of knowledge, where the unruly body meets unruled knowledge, we insist not just on representation but on pleasure, challenging traditional academic forms (cf. Brueggemann 2023, 77).

> My father told me: 'Anger is a luxury that we cannot afford.'
> Be composed, calm, still – laugh when they ask you
> smile when they talk, answer them,
> educate them.
> This is why we dance,
> Because if I speak, I'm dangerous
> (El-Kurd 2018)

When we speak truthfully, we are dangerous. So we become at once polyglots and mind-readers. We read in their handwriting and gestures how plainly we can talk, and we tame our anger. Being transparent, being 'clear' in our endeavour to live meaningful lives, becomes nothing short of forced emotional, biographical and community exhibitionism.

To be normal would be to be transparent, to be clear, to be explained. That way, we can be integrated with ease into what exists already. Epistemological justice, then, cannot emerge from violence that expects the labour of self-dociling to make us conform to forms and definitions of rigour that perpetuate violence and eat away at our sanity. Of course they do. These are rubrics developed to enable colonisation, justify marginalisation and enact dehumanisation – instead, I dream of a *rigour* intended to heal, remediate and enliven.

Thriving at the limits of reason means that we encode our plain thoughts into a dance of words and ideas that our kin recognises, that is healing to us, that is the kind of writing that we need. However, such emancipated writing feels alien to those seeking to observe us from the outside or understand us in a detached manner. How we move, how we breathe, how we write and *are*, that is *us*. To our past selves, and those affected by the above, we say: learn how to see your writing not as a matter in-itself, but as a witness and echo of our being-as-dance. That is the context from which we will begin our journey.

Movement II: Normalcy

The limits of reasons are the margins.
Occupy the margins and make them habitable.
Create sanctuaries there and thrive in *the other*.

This text is dedicated to ourselves and our peers, navigating lives beyond the moulds of the standard and the default. This exploration probes the logical outcomes that manifest when one is forced or compelled to dwell at the intersection of institutional rigidity and our unyielding will to thrive. Compelled to call *home*, where reason fails to serve. If, due to our biography and heritage – our accumulated knowledge and assets – we find ourselves and our histories alienated within academic settings, a battleground of difference is carved into our psyches.

Stigma here is not only a symptom or by-product of extractionist-capitalist exploitation systems; it is an extension of them. Stigma becomes/is the noxious co-conspirator of corporations and bureaucracy to shame self-care, disincentivise boundary-setting, and disgrace rest. These ‘stigma machines’ (Tyler 2020) have commodified our mental wellbeing to fuel capitalism, effectively marginalising the global majority in particular. At the core of this marginalisation is our enforced role as epistemological outsiders: unaccepted, not at home, merely existing as hybrids.

The state of being choiceless in this intersection is profound. Positioned at the margins by our origins and by factors beyond our control, we cannot escape our biographies, or how our personal and collective histories are interpreted by those in power. However, we can scrutinise this otherness. Our proximity to this otherness, our historical grounding here, and our deep familiarity with marginality, empower us to discuss it with native fluency. While those from the centre may visit, we claim the margins as our home. Here, we must establish our dwellings: not easy homes, but ours nonetheless. Even if we depart, maintaining complex connections with these origins, *Heimat* – a profound sense of home – remains steadfast, no matter the distance, temporal or geographical. *Heimat* fails to translate well. Its nuance is not captured with 'home', 'parent-land' or 'homeland'. It is rootedness and commitment at once. It may be essentialist or constructivist, both, or neither; it just is what it is. *Heimat* is evident, and while it may not be easy, for better or worse, it is unambiguous. Unlike the academy, where belonging feels conditional, revocable and contingent.

Particularly troubling is the academic sphere's detrimental impact on queer and Brown lives through what we identify as a misapplication of academic rigour. This misappropriation manifests in privileging their own epistemologies over others, undermining the diverse ways of knowing that we bring to the ivory tower, that *they* desperately lack. That which they do not know. That which they don't even know they do not know. The academic medium must become conducive to our modes of expression and knowledge, allowing us to be read and evaluated through frameworks that valorise our unique contributions.

The stigmatisation referenced by Tyler (2020) pertains to the deadening of lived richness and the normativity of linear textual thinking, in the name of what is considered rigorous. Yet *their* rigour is so narrow in scope, it feels like a caricature at best, or maybe pure maleficence.

We critique paradoxes tied to expectations for linear and clear language in academia, illustrating why these demands are unattainable for those from the margins. Neutralisation, scientification, abstraction and the disruptive decontextualisation through the academic mode produce similar injustices (Reardon and Tallbear 2012). The perseverance of '[relegating] indigenous knowing to the realm of culture or mere belief' (Reardon and Tallbear 2012, S233). Our knowing is intertwined with our existence – how we move, breathe, see, listen, speak and are, as well as the very bodies we inhabit. Just as our DNA carries the stories of our ancestors, reducing these to mere medical or molecular components overlooks the breadth of these narratives. It is about nothing less than redrawing boundaries of context, which means, in specific cases, to get to an 'Understanding [of our] genetics as a storytelling practice', S234). Inclusive hermeneutics must recognise genetics as a form of inherited knowledge, a form of intangible property that demands new forms of storytelling to appreciate it with justice. Without this recognition, the knowledges of our ancestors that reside materially in us will remain misunderstood.

Will it be hard to write in such a fashion? 'Why is it so damn hard to write?' Perhaps because we have unlearnt to speak our native tongues? Perhaps it is because we were never meant to be written; we were meant to dance.

What we are left to do is twofold: We are forced into doublespeak with disadvantage – and are driven into exhaustion. Writing at the limits of reason means to write against language and to demand that our invisible labour be recognised as academically valuable, by the very academy that establishes and perpetuates asymmetrical power relationships under the guise of neutrality, unbiasedness, peer review, accountability and integrity. We assert our dignity in a manner that is essential, not self-indulgent; transformative, not merely self-referential. We are tasked with bending the prelingual into the treacherous ground of language, the backstabbing halls of the academy, the oppressive tools we are bound to while we fight for acceptance within the master's house. How can one compose calm treatises or argumentations when surrounded by epistemological adversaries in halls that still reek of epistemi$^{\text{pesti}}_{\text{cides}}$?

Recognise this: writing is in fact *not* hard. Writing is like dance, it is in our blood. Writing like *them*, though, that is what is hard. The contortions and mind games that happen in our heads before the writing, and on the pages once the text stands. Our bodies, environments and minds signify differently to you and/or the other.

The oceans represent a space to anchor oneself (Kauanui 2015), mirroring the morphologies of islands that resemble our minds. To outsiders, the territories from which we hail might seem unorganised, lacking a governance structure that appears sensible (Kauanui 2015). However, such aesthetic appraisals carry the normative forces and normalising violence inherent in any cross-cultural judgement. Normativity is imposed through expectations of certain forms of self-governance and the recognition of specific patterns and institutions. When external observers fail to see enough of themselves in us, delegitimisation occurs. Yet, it is the absence of knowledge among our judges that leads them to misunderstand, misread or overlook our systems of recognition and expression. Their lack of local knowledge and contextual understanding results in incorrect decisions, delegitimising alternative ways of knowing and obstructing an equitable exchange of knowledge; to educate those who lack understanding. Our knowledge is proudly Oceanic, which reflects not only a geographical and geological phenomenology, but also permeates my body, influencing how we see, who we are and how we move; I too am Oceanic and fluid in my perception and expression (cf. Ingersoll 2016). However, Oceanic knowing will remain elusive to those who feel comfortable only on land.

Our attempts to write about life and for the living are hindered by the linear, conventional and precedent-based modes of knowing that dominate academic discourse. The 'thesis', as it currently stands, recognises only a fraction of legitimate and worthy ways of knowing. This pursuit of rigour and proficiency often stifles possibilities and raises doubts and regrets, disproportionately impacting marginalised communities – my community, my friends, peers, allies, ancestors and kin, and those who are missing.

The irony is that the academy misunderstands its own medium of expression. Textuality is deceptive. Texts are not stable, not unchanging constructs, not immutable at all. Instead, they are dynamic, entangled, ever-changing and quasi-fluid. *Oceanic* really. Since every reading, every hermeneutic, depends on the reader, context, moment and many other factors – with each new reading being a novel encounter – textuality itself should be understood as a heterotemporal dislocative medium: a medium that is neither temporally nor semiotically stable, but is constantly changing in its agency, politics, appellative content and signification; that is not located in a single space or medium, but all-encompassing and mobile. Context, readers, geography and language inevitably change, thereby profoundly affecting all that is written, and in turn, the dance of new meanings continues, and knowing *moves*.

Any writing is a sensory trace of embodied experiences. Joshi (2022) discusses the 'poetic persona' as a vital tool in storytelling, necessary for addressing the challenges of expressing what is essentially sensory. Viewing textuality as a non-sensory experience is to misunderstand the medium. Viewing textuality as a mono-locative, unidirectional flow of information is to misunderstand the medium. Viewing textuality as a temporally or geographically unique instance is to vehemently misunderstand the medium. Writing is Oceanic, writing is dance. In our writing, we dance, and you must too. Dance dangerously, rigorously, and with the power of occupying the margins of reason, unbridled and like the Ocean.

Writing is not merely a sensory medium; it is an embodied one. The true site of textuality is not the page, but the mind, the brain, the body, the skin – in other words, the visceral and the affective. As textuality itself, through technological innovations, becomes disrupted, the envelope of where writing is located transforms and expands further. The resonating body of textuality where text 'happens' remains the body, the mind and the affect, but the actuators of textuality extend to comprise complicated and distributed network technologies. In this textual dance, no participant is tame – neither language, reader, text, nor ink (or pixels) themselves are docile. All ravage each other in an unstable dance, struggling to grasp that which is inherently elusive. How does this relate to the liminality of reason?

To hear a poem is to experience its momentary escape from the prison cell of the page, where silence is enforced, to a freedom dependent only on the ability to open one's mouth – that most democratic of instruments – and speak (Collins 2003, 3).

Emancipatory forms seek to explicitly destabilise language. Detachment and non-affectedness privilege those who write about but are not affected, disenfranchising those seeking self-actualisation and emancipation. It is necessary to declare which communities are vulnerable to attack, as this form of erasure is inextricably tied to the medium of writing. We aim to reclaim language, framings and contexts. How we write, and how we assume writing should appear, becomes a political question with profound implications for power, justice, inclusion and the right to thrive.

Agamben, in his *Sacrament of Language* (2018), posits that the oath, a special form of language, bridges the sacred/legal and the profane, anchoring the promise of certainty that governs sociality. Echoing this, apocryphally, playwright Tom Stoppard is said to have claimed that 'Law is just poetry enforced by the police'. This insight sharpens its relevance where conventional language and its frameworks only partially accommodate the realities of those at the margins. The constrained nature of academic form – a misappropriation of academic rigour, we argue – disproportionately marginalises queer and Brown lives at the expense of established norms. Yet, it is within these very margins that the pulsating heart of life and knowledge exists, where theory breathes and language inevitably falters.

Progressing through our chapter, we propose new forms not merely through descriptive exposition but through active enactment and demonstration. Our intent is not to dissect theory, but to vividly display it, challenging the confines of accepted academic form, broadening the envelope of what can be imagined, and for teaching to become legible-as-healing. This endeavour is not merely for the sake of innovation but to earnestly serve those who will be enlivened through academic practice that is vibrant, of life, and embedded in the communities we are a part of.

The current formal scholarly form, deeply ritualised and contextual as it stands today, represents only the latest iteration in a long history of academic knowledge dissemination. As Shapin (1995) and Shapin and Schaffer (2011) argue, transparency and accountability were assured through transparent logical and scientific accuracy, as well as through social constructions of trustworthiness grounded in independent wealth and gentility, which were only obtainable by specific elites. Today's form of scientific publication is just as much a product of our contemporary cultural constructions, and far from a quasi-divine epistemological certainty (De Sousa Santos 2014). Despite the allure of stability and unwavering certainty of our institutions, academic forms do evolve, adapt, change, are fluid and become revised, and *can* embrace new modes of knowing (Ladson-Billings 2014). Yet, institutional change is often sluggish, encountering implicit or explicit resistance, appearing superfluous to those well-served by the status quo.

Snorton and Yapp (2020) poignantly enquire: 'For those historically excluded, what expectations surround these individuals when they enter an institution?' It is those in power, comfortable within the established system, who often obstruct, overlook or outright oppose necessary changes (hooks 1994).

But it is in the subaltern way of speaking that our ability to trace, sense and identify instances of marginalisation, and in particular White supremacy at the expense of Blackness, and therein Female Blackness.

'The power of this speech is not simply that it enables resistance to White supremacy, but also that it forges a space for alternative cultural production and alternative epistemologies – different ways of thinking and knowing that were crucial to creating a counter-hegemonic worldview ... When I asked an ethnically diverse group of students in a course I was teaching on Black woman writers why we heard standard English spoken in the classroom, they were momentarily speechless' (hooks 1994, 171).

The types of knowledge and knowing that are emancipatory and necessary to address our holistic challenges are themselves holistic and consuming. We are discussing not only knowledge of the living but knowledge that is in itself alive.

As we see with Foucault, as the episteme changes it is also the very nature of what is considered 'knowledge' that is transformed, not just what is known but also what is knowable. Haraway expands this conceptualisation of knowledge and knowing, by weaving in material companions, living humans and nonhumans, into networked epistemologies of mutual recognition and kinship. Post-cyborgian kinships as forms of knowing emancipates material and inherited categories for communities of collective values and interest (Haraway 2008; Foucault 2005). These theorists enable us to challenge and resist the promises of normalising taxonomies of thought to order the world. The redrawing of taxonomies of thought through transgression is an involuntary necessity of queer life and living. Queer lives are political, not by choice, but through their nature. It is not queer life that seeks to haunt politics, but politics that cannot but haunt queer life.

> I like to write from memory, as incomplete of a record as this provides. (Levin et al. 1998, 162)

Yet, the critique of the written form is inherently bound by the forms of academic writing, as Michel Foucault explores in 'What is an Author?' (Foucault 1979). The urgency with which we yearn for innovation and leniency above all in thesis, reflects our witnessing of our peers and applicants who struggle with the contradictory nature of this form – its intrinsic contradictions of form and function, content and constraints. The ivory tower's imposition of its taxonomies of knowing, at the expense of lived knowledge, epitomises this struggle (Foucault 2005).

> I write from memory, with the authority of experience, from the heart and from a place of necessity. I write because it is required. That is what you are looking at. (We here now)

Rigour is not heartlessness. Questions of purity of methodology loom large, and yet they seem so theological to me, when my objective is not the divine, but to preserve life and the living. These precious texts off the margins must be understood as alive, not as deadened, archivable scriptures. This necessitates a handwriting usable both in the field and on placards, bridging art, the vulgar, the mundane, the popular and academia. These distinctions, while useful to maintain the status quo and uphold hierarchies, restrict us from acknowledging the wisdom from below – the citations of the streets, the references from the forest or the bibliographies of the dreamt (cf. Kamunge et al 2018).

We were never meant to write; we were meant to dance. Each of us has unique ways of expressing ourselves that may not align easily with writing. This misalignment is aggravated by the state of these intellectual spaces and media we seek to express ourselves in, as they are compromised sites that reek of inaccessibility, unwelcome occupation and oppression. When we close our eyes, we feel that we were never meant to write, but to dance, yearning for a physical and spontaneous mode of expression that writing could never be – at least not writing how we learnt it within the academy. We yearn for forms that allow for the externalisation of emotions and moods in more direct and visceral ways than textuality can provide.

Human communication is a kaleidoscope of language, body, voice, gestures, facial expressions, timbre and accent. Dance and other forms of bodily expression offer a pathway that may feel more natural and freeing, unbridled from the restrictive corset of the corpus of written textuality. Emancipated from these, we may feel more at ease and at home in somatic and embodied expressive forms, where we can be free, as these forms may convey what words inherently cannot.

Movement III: Synthesis of the dancing writer at the limits of reason

Ultimately, both writing and dance are powerful mediums of human expression, each with its own challenges and beauties. The key might be in finding the form of expression that best aligns with one's inner self in a manner that allows one to communicate in the most authentic and fulfilling way. A vision of writing that is driven by affect and a rigour of intuition, a commitment to context, not to convention. For those of us with the wisdom of the marginalised, this means navigating and negotiating with systems and structures that have not always recognised or valued our voices and stories.

Without the constraints of textuality, dance or other forms of art offer more natural or freeing affordances of expression. While writing requires the translation of thinking, ideas, concepts and feelings into a symbolic system of language with an existing and established firm reference framework, danced modes of writing express through movement, possibly echoing older forms of human communication that preceded the development of written language. Our stories, deeply entwined with our bodies, who or how we love, imbued with embodied knowing or inherited intergenerational or ancestral wisdom and oral tradition, find fuller expression in these alternative modalities. For those of us with inherited knowledges, finding expression that aligns with our inner self, that allows us to communicate in the most authentic and fulfilling way, means navigating systems and structures that have not always valued or recognised our voices and stories.

Language is a technology and, like any technology, it is not only a means of expression but is also constituted with values, inequalities and powers of the societies that use it. For minorities in particular, this means that we are not entering the domain of language on an equal playing field. Language (especially if it is the language of the other, of the dominant, of the colonisers or power-holders or system architects) is inherently treacherous. Language itself has been framed as a domain from which we are excluded, or where we are merely considered visitors, learners, foreigners, or throughfare; but never *Home, Resident, Native, or In Charge*. Our participation in language itself is subject to appraisal; not taken for granted. In the backdrop of all this, a reluctance or mistrust of language cannot be surprising or our fault.

We are entitled to yearn and seek to invoke other forms of knowledge and expression that have been devalued by an epistemology dominated by the narrowly written and the irresponsibly rational. Sometimes, even merely expressing the absence of the validity of reason, or the utter failures of an adequate language to express our lifeworlds, is all we draw attention to. And that itself is good enough. In the absence of full recognition, appellative dance and other forms of bodily expression must be valued and celebrated as meaningful in their own right, as part of the project of learning to speak with power, to communicate experiences, emotions and knowledge that challenge the limitations of reason and the power structures that support it. For us, this assertion is a reminder of the diverse and rich ways in which our ancestors have communicated and preserved knowledge, often in the face of efforts to silence or erase them; alternative forms of expression and knowledge, recognising the richness and depth they can bring to our understanding of the world. This is a critical step towards ensuring that our voices are not just included but are central to the narratives and discourses that shape our world.

Dance, like writing, can be reimagined as a space of resistance and empowerment, where our voices find ways to express themselves and be heard on our terms, challenging dominant narratives and constructing new ways to understand and inhabit the world. For us, this is not merely an academic or theoretical exercise but a lived reality and an ongoing struggle for recognition, dignity and justice. This understanding expands the realms of how we express and see ourselves, positioning dance not just as an act but as a philosophy and way of being, thinking and retaining sovereignty over modes of expression and dwelling in a manner that brings us joy. Writing as an extenuation of dance, when faced with oppressive reason, becomes a fundamental aspect of existence and an assertion of resistance. This is a call to break the norms that seek to dismantle us, to liberate ourselves from *their* rigidity, and to define and assert our existence with any means possible. It's a declaration that our narratives, our stories and our truths are not to be bound by the conventional structures that have historically sought to constrain us. In grappling with these issues, we are not merely engaged in an academic exercise but in a lived reality, an ongoing struggle for recognition, dignity and justice. Here, dance transcends being a mere method of expression – it becomes the expression itself, a vibrant testament to our collective becoming and the reimagining of spaces where marginalised voices find ways to express themselves and be heard.

References

Agamben, Giorgio. 2018. *The Sacrament of Language: An archaeology of the oath*. Weinheim: Wiley.

Brueggemann, MJ 2023. 'Send in the Clowns: Scoping non-representational theory as ally and method to foster inclusiveness in digital innovation', PhD thesis, Lancaster University. Accessed 1 April 2025. https://ualresearchonline.arts.ac.uk/id/eprint/21586/1/RepoPhD_MJHBrueggemann.pdf.

Collins, Billy. 2003. 'Poems in the air'. In *The Spoken Word Revolution: Slam, hip-hop and the poetry of a new generation*, edited by Mark Eleveld, 3–5. Naperville, IL: Sourcebooks.

De Sousa Santos, Boaventura. 2014. *Epistemologies of the South: Justice against epistemicide*. Boulder, CO: Paradigm Publishers.

El-Kurd, Mohammed. 2018. 'This is why we dance'. Accessed 1 April 2025. https://mapsforteeth.com/2018/05/15/mohammed-el-kurd/.

Foucault, Michel. 1979 [1969]. 'What is an author?', *Screen* 20(1): 13–34. https://doi.org/10.1093/screen/20.1.13.

Foucault, Michel. 2005. *The Order of Things*. Chicago: Routledge.

Haraway, D. J. 2008. *When Species Meet*. Minneapolis: University of Minnesota Press.

Hogg, Meghan. 2020. 'Mad for fat: Toward a queer politics of embodied difference', *Knots: An undergraduate journal of disability studies* 5(1): 71–86.

hooks, bell. 1994. *Teaching to Transgress: Education as the practice of freedom*. New York: Routledge.

Ingersoll, Karin Amimoto. 2016. *Waves of Knowing: A seascape epistemology*. Durham, NC: Duke University Press.

Joshi, Anushree. 2022. 'The voice in twenty-first century spoken word poetry and confessionalism: An analysis of performances by Lozada-Oliva, Benaim and Vaid-Menon', *Women's Studies* 51(1): 70–87.

Kamunge, Beth, Wambui Mwangi and Osop Abdi Ali. 2018. 'Writing in the Fire Now: Beth dialogues with Wambui and Osop'. In *The Fire Now: Anti-racist scholarship in times of explicit racial violence*, edited by Azeezat Johnson, Remi Joseph-Salisbury and Beth Kamunge, 189–97. London: Zed Books.

Kauanui, J. Kehaulani. 2015. 'Imperial ocean: The Pacific as a critical site for American studies', *American Quarterly* 67(3): 625–36.

Ladson-Billings, Gloria. 2014. 'Culturally relevant pedagogy 2.0: a.k.a. the remix', *Harvard Educational Review* 84(1): 74–84.

Levin, Janna, Evan Scannapieco, Giancarlo de Gasperis, Joseph Silk and John D. Barrow. 1998. 'How the universe got its spots', *Physical Review D* 58(12): 123006-1–123006-4.

Miserandino, Christine. 2017 [2003]. 'The spoon theory'. In *Beginning with Disability: A primer*, edited by Lennard J. Davis, 174–8. New York: Routledge.
Reardon, Jenny and Kim Tallbear. 2012. '"Your DNA is our history": Genomics, anthropology, and the construction of whiteness as property', *Current Anthropology* 53(S5): S233–45.
Shapin, Steven. 1995. *A Social History of Truth: Civility and science in seventeenth-century England*. Chicago: University of Chicago Press.
Shapin, Steven and Simon Schaffer. 2011. *Leviathan and the Air-Pump: Hobbes, Boyle, and the experimental life*. Princeton, NJ: Princeton University Press.
Snorton, C. R. and H. Yapp. 2020. '"Sensuous contemplation": thinking race at its saturation points'. In *Saturation: Race, art, and the circulation of value*, edited by C. Riley Snorton and Hentyle Yapp, 1–12. Cambridge, MA: MIT Press.
Tyler, Imogen. 2020. *Stigma: The machinery of inequality*. London: Bloomsbury.
Wolframe, PhebeAnn Marjory. 2013. 'The madwoman in the academy, or revealing the invisible straightjacket: Theorising and teaching saneism and sane privilege', *Disability Studies Quarterly* 33(1). https://doi.org/10.18061/dsq.v33i1.3425.

Appendix 1: Workflow for duckyfuzz encoding tool for chapter text

1. Text Preprocessing:
   The input text is tokenised into individual words, converted to lowercase and filtered to retain only alphabetic tokens. This step prepares the text for further processing by removing punctuation and irrelevant characters.
   Each token is then lemmatised – words are reduced to their base or root form, for standardisation.
2. Seed Generation:
   A seed for randomisation is generated, based on the current timestamp or latitude/longitude, so output can be replicated with the same seed.
3. Rhyme Grouping:
   Creates a mapping of words to their potential rhymes, which will be used later to modify the poem's lines.
4. Token Shuffling:
   The tokens are shuffled randomly to create a varied structure in the generated poem, ensuring that the output does not follow the original order of the input text.
5. Poem Generation:
   The script constructs the poem by iterating through a specified number of stanzas and lines per stanza. For each line a random number of tokens is selected to form the line. If the last token of the line has a rhyme in the rhyme groups, it is replaced with a randomly chosen rhyme, adding a phonetic element to the output.
6. Phonetic Segmentation with DMetaphone algorithm:

The Double Metaphone algorithm generates phonetic representations of words, enabling analysis based on sound rather than spelling, and thus allowing identification of similar-sounding words.

The script processes input text, finding the closest words from the neologism list. It:

- takes an input word and generates its double metaphone representation (a phonetic encoding)
- compares this representation with the metaphone representations of words in the neologism list
- calculates similarity based on the overlap of phonetic components, allowing it to identify words that sound similar to the input word.

7. Word Replacement with Neologisms:

After generating the initial poem, the script replaces words in the poem with words from a provided list of neologisms, that I previously generated using custom built neural networks. This part is done using a metaphone similarity function, which finds phonetically similar words based on their sounds rather than their spellings.

Link to neologisms dataset – https://github.com/koundinyad/neologisms.txt.

Appendix 2: duckyfuzz encoded text

Time-based encoding of the chapter text

threautt whoich threautt mccliobly whiists braask wointly wointly
rhierth sqoary gloorn
yeably ferst reaurk
hraosts gruintz hypiaoms
geaungly plurn pourts wointly pourts bloongs foorth
yoark flierm vuiengly
yuency wointly pourts wointly
rhierth snourt freongly heorf yoark dynof flaiosk
yoark yeuw yuff schmuoty vuiengly

tseung wointly thrieft yoark gruintz shoups
mcaests whausch psycheidy wointly chroupt mccrougy
typeusly wointly yoark speurth schnef whiists hraosts spriants
mcmadly wointly hyuow whiists hraosts wointly rhierth
mccraerm wointly yoark bloongs geaungly threautt vuiengly

heorf whiists pourts geaungly
wointly wointly speurth wointly bloongs
yuff sneiapt whausch wointly wointly wueng
whiists friountz wointly rhierth treemp

yoark whiists threautt geaungly speurth pfaurn speurth hydrauepp
yoark wointly bloongs
threautt friountz typeusly mcnaobs theaunts yuff mcmadly
whausch wointly hraosts heorf cruiedy
reaurk yuff geaungly bloongs threautt pliaght symbuiers
freongly braask wointly typeusly wointly whiists yuff gleaunt
hraosts hraosts yuff wointly bloongs
rhierth wointly geently wheungs scruatz yeuw creiz snourt'creiz
whiists sciaogy schroast gleaunt

yuency wheialls hraosts freongly wointly wointly draif yeably
yuff mcaests hraosts whiists whiists bloew
yuff heorf vuiengly
yuff beuntz whausch speurth whausch pourts
speurth spriants vuiengly rhierth hraosts typeusly schmuoty shoups
wointly chroupt reaurk rhierth
wheorth whiists wointly yuff whausch mccraerm geupt bloew
bloongs hraosts wiisk mcclierth rhierth
bloongs wointly sniourk pourts mcniaongly haiongly whausch geaungly

yoark yeuw wointly beuntz
thoonk yuff yuff bloongs rhierth
whiists whiists bloongs wointly kraitts draif schnef
heorf pourts hraosts tseung whiists heorf wiourth schlaiarf
whiists mccreauv pfeuls schneaulls yoark pfiecy
wheungs yoark wointly
whausch snaiodly sneaurm bloongs whausch
threautt schwiungly mcmadly bloongs
fluoght hraosts mccreauv wointly rhierth pourts

braask wointly whiists speurth yeuw mcniaongly
thoonk mcnaobs rhierth hypaangly symbaangs
wointly yoark hypiaoms whausch wheialls wointly pourts braask
yoark hraosts yeuw floently
mcnaobs wointly whiists gleaunt fliamp
gloorn whauert bloew

brounn wointly beuntz whaunts
mcmadly psycheidy wointly gleaunt floently whiists shoups
mckieuntly rhierth hraosts rhierth hydraiogy schnerk whiists

Space-based encoding of the chapter text

rhierth hypiaoms gleaunt whausch
hraosts bloongs sniourk wointly hyoiangs
bloongs whiists wiourth mcniaongly
whaunts dynof yeuw whiists rhierth
hyoiangs threautt speurth pleisk hydreund
braask mcmadly wointly
froubs hraosts mccreauv schniought snourt
bleurds draif mciert
pheops hydreund synieurg yuff wointly hroems.

mccreauv yuency whausch mcmadly
mcmadly whiists braask dynorm wointly bloongs
yoark mcclierth mcaests mcaests'
braask schwiungly cruiedy yeuw gleaunt reaurk
snourt whiists rhierth gloorn speurth fends
typeusly wointly bloongs wointly mciert
whaiath mccloeld giaontz
whiists yoark hydraiaz smiously joids
whiists gleaunt jualy

wointly geaungly jualy
yoark hyuow reaurk
rhierth hraosts gloorn
wiourth yeorn whiists wointly rhierth chroupt
rhierth jaady wheungs snourt
wointly mccraonn symbuiers yuff gleaunt typeusly
whiists whiists srauells wointly whiists mcaests
wointly hraosts whuirm
rhierth bloongs typeusly geaungly yuff waioms

rhierth pourts snourt hraosts wointly fruigs
floently typeusly yeorn speurth psycheidy
wointly braask pourts friountz
hraosts whausch wointly reaurk
rhierth whoept wiisk smiountz bloongs

whausch heorf braask reaurk
yoark hraosts greiadly braask rhierth
pliaght whausch pleisk
whiists whausch hraosts whausch stuirly

hraosts khieft ferst
schmuoty freongly yeuw vuiengly pourts bloongs
vuiengly whausch rhierth yoark sqoary
woongs gleaunt yuff whausch'vuiengly
yuff rhierth chroupt mccraerm wointly hydreund
sneaurm schnerk hraosts
yoark snourt rhierth pfeuls
whausch braask whausch pfell hraosts
mcniaongly speurth reaurk

yuff bloongs snourt
joids whiists threautt gedly
hyuow snourt whausch hraosts hraosts
rhierth yeuw mcmadly threautt vuiengly
synieurg wointly wointly yuency
hraosts wointly hydreund
wointly pourts yoark shraigy wauerk schmiings
bloongs mccruiebs wointly braask srauells geaungly
rhierth hraosts reaurk hydraiams schneaulls

9

The smell of rain on hot concrete

Kerry McInerney

It is much too late for the accounts of death to prevent other deaths; and it is much too early for such scenes of death to halt other crimes. But in the meantime, in the space of the interval, between too late and too early, between the no longer and the not yet, our lives are coeval with the girl's in the as-yet-incomplete project of freedom. In the meantime, it is clear that her life and ours hang in the balance.

Saidiya Hartman, 'Venus in two acts' (2008, 14)

***

Water is forbidden in the archives. Despite this, I can't stop myself from crying over the documents. I have to tilt my face away, lest they are marked by my emotional excess. I was told that the archives would be cold, but my thirst radiates outwards. I feel my tongue thickening in my mouth. I can't afford to lose any more water here, and yet I sweat, and I cry.

These pages are too dry. As I turn each page, I hear them whispering against one another. I imagine them making love, their skin velvety soft as vellum. I intrude on their intimacy. I wait for them to speak, but I am as foreign to them as they are to me. They curdle under the oil of my skin. I handle the books carefully, supporting their damaged spines with foam blocks. Alone, they cannot bear the weight of their own words.

In their essay 'Violence, mourning, politics', Judith Butler writes: 'We're undone by each other. And if we're not, we're missing something. This seems so clearly the case with grief, but this can be so only because it was already the case with desire. One does not always stay intact. It may be that one wants to, or does, but it may also be that despite one's best efforts, one is undone, in the face of the other, by the touch, by the scent, by the feel, by the prospect of the touch, by the memory of the feel' (Butler 2003, 13).

As I undo these documents to read them, I am, time and time again, undone by them. When I read a particularly visceral account of force-feeding in Holloway prison, my body, unprompted, would start to retch in sympathy. The dirt from the pages crusts on my fingers. At one point, I cut myself on the corner of a file. The blood welled, dark and bulbous. In that moment, I was not afraid for myself but rather for the documents. That the pages would consume this droplet of myself and that they would be irretrievably changed by my blood, my tears, my abject excess.

In *Powers of Horror: An essay on abjection*, Julia Kristeva posits that blood, urine, faeces, vomit, spit, breastmilk, all things fluid and bodily, are a horrifying affront to the individual's sense of self as an autonomous, discrete, bounded creature. The body turns inside out: 'the body's inside, in that case, shows up in order to compensate for the collapse of the border between inside and outside. It is as if the skin, a fragile container, no longer guaranteed the integrity of one's "own and clean self" but, scraped or transparent, invisible or taut, gave way before the dejection of its contents. Urine, blood, sperm, excrement then show up in order to reassure a subject that is lacking its "own and clean self"' (Kristeva 1982, 53). She terms this experience of the breakdown between inside and outside, subject and object, the abject: 'it is thus not lack of cleanliness or health that causes abjection but what disturbs identity, system, order. What does not respect borders, positions, rules. The in-between, the ambiguous, the composite' (Kristeva 1982, 4).

As I work to sort, quantify, code and process the documents I encounter in the archive, the documents themselves reject this easy delineation between self and other. I start to carry these words and these stories with me, long after the archive closes. In her work on the prison writings of hunger strikers, *The Hunger Artists: Starving, writing and imprisonment*, Maud Ellmann foregrounds the 'savage loneliness' of pain, hunger, and other bodily experiences (Ellmann 1993, 6). It echoes Elaine Scarry's influential thesis, that pain destroys human language, taking us back to a prelinguistic state: this, in Scarry's view, makes torture a literally world-destroying experience. But Ellmann insists that the writings of prisoners transform the loneliness of hunger, of pain, into a shared act of protest. Moreover, Ellmann argues, during the hunger strike there is an inverse relationship between bodily consumption and the verbal or written production of words. As I sift through their diaries, letters, newspaper clippings, I gain a strange familiarity with the loved ones of others. Instead, their histories settle and sediment upon my skin. My spine splinters beneath their weight.

But when I try to imagine my own loved ones, my own ancestors, here in this archive, their embrace escapes me. Sometimes I try to imagine a different archive of my family's memories. Pages upon pages filled with the sweet heat of chilli, the bitter bite of burnt cumin, the beat of the drums against my tongue, against a wide and deep and mellow sky. I excavate my flesh to find an archive of the everyday violence of living. But if the past is another country, it seems that my family left that one too. I feel this swelling wave of dust and silence. And I wait. I wait for it to break.

***

Perhaps the archive is no place for my family, because I do not have a family tree. I have a family sea. It rushes, salty and ferrous, through my veins. My body and theirs are too fluid for the genealogical method. Something thicker and darker than blood or water binds us. Something like molasses, or treacle. Sticky, inescapable, sweet and bitter all at once.

I lived on a boat, as a child, for two years. I slowly battled against nausea to become sea-hardy, only to find that when I walked on land again, the ground tilted. I suffered from land-sickness. While its physical effects wore off after a couple of minutes, it took another two years before I could make my home on land again.

These are the oceanic histories I want to remember. There are others I want to forget. I try not to think of my settler ancestors, hungrily traversing the seas. The people they treated as cargo. I try not to think about the colonial genealogies that play out upon my skin. I try not to think about a girl called shame who has my face. For years, I feel like a smooth, dark round of hardboiled aniseed: sweet and salty and achingly sad. I think of myself as an acquired taste.

Like any liquid, I take the shape of whatever container I am placed in. Deleuze and Guattari say that bastard and mixed blood are the true names of race (Deleuze and Guattari 2004). But I was raced and unraced and erased. I think of all the single tick-boxes used to disclose my ethnicity, and I think: you did such violence to me. I think of the name I would have received, if my parents had not been frightened that I would be bullied. I roll it around my mouth, but it tastes like foreign candy. I am still too estranged from who I could have been. I see White people named after their grandparents, their great-grandparents, and think that we would need so many more children to bear the names of our dead.

In a spate of curious googling, I find out that the Māori word for land – *whenua* – is the same word for placenta (Royal 2007). I feel like I am ogling something precious. The land feeds us and nourishes us like the placenta in the womb. The land itself is understood to be the placenta of Papatūānuku, the earth goddess. In this womb of a world we are sustained by her afterbirth. After a human baby is born, the placenta is buried, so that earth returns to earth. I wish that I could feel so tethered to the earth. Clearly my placenta was not buried. Post-birth, my last tether was severed and I was set adrift, the placenta placed in a basket and sent out to sea. I dream of all those afterbirths putting down roots. I dream of those roots binding the land together, holding it firm in the face of a storm. I dream of a basket tossed by the waves.

***

prometheus

i received poetry on
the wingtips of grief

if life is the oil spill,
poetry is its iridescence.

i thought that was the price
of brilliance; peace, ripped from

my body like a pulsating
organ. foolishly, I thought

it would grow back again.
it was painfully cliché,

that loss of innocence. i was
a bad victim and resented

their herculean rescue
efforts. i lost my stomach

for being good; it was
always bound to ruin me;

i thought i was eternal fire,
but i was only kindling.

***

Figure 9.1 *Prometheus*, by Lucy Smith, 2024. *Source*: © 2024 Lucy Smith.

During the COVID-19 pandemic, I became obsessed with archiving. I felt a compulsive need to document – through academic writing and through art – the way that certain spaces had become alien to me. I became scared to leave the house, frightened to walk to work, terrified of how my face or my body would be read by an outsider – as a virus or a pathogen, whether COVID-19 or something else much more racialised and nebulous. I felt overexposed, visible, like a raw nerve or a bleeding gum. Yet, at the same time, I felt silent and helpless. How could I explain this rising wave of anxiety to my colleagues and my friends, or even my family?

In *White Sight*, Nicholas Mirzoeff analyses how the White gaze actively produces the parameters of what people are able to see, and codifies this narrow space as the only existing plane of reality: 'the visual politics and practices of Whiteness nonetheless seek to create a time and space such that people identifying as White can act as if their reality is all there is … These layered relations of force produce White sight as a hierarchy, at once racializing and patriarchal, which is then projected onto external reality. It is "real" in that it constrains and shapes experience every day, but it is not equally experienced, let alone simply "true"' (Mirzoeff 2023, 4).

To bear witness is to see, and yet we know that racism is rendered literally imperceptible. The White supremacist world that we live in makes racial experiences possible, and yet paradoxically, it also makes these very same racial experiences illegible, unspeakable, insensible and impossible. I struggled for so long to find a lexicon to express my own sense of normality. I only possessed the vocabulary to talk about what was perceived as the 'unexpected', the singular act of violence, the breaching of the peaceful, sea-like, sensuous norm that was then quickly and quietly absorbed back beneath the surface.

The enormity of that challenge silenced me. How do you name the ocean? And how do you do so when the island we all live on is taken to be a never-ending continent, an ever-spreading land mass that leaves no space for naming the waters that surround us? How do you name the ocean? How do you name the living, breathing, watery mass that threatens to overwhelm us? How do you name the ocean? How do you name that which will not let you breathe?

This is the problem with bearing witness. To bear means to remember, but the ocean drank away our memories long ago. One day, my mother and I were cooking and she mentioned that there is a Cantonese word that describes the smoky flavour when food is seared at high heat in the wok. The problem was that most of our language had trickled away. Holding onto words felt like cupping our hands to hold onto water. Soon, all we had left was the memory of wetness, running in careless rivulets around my mother's wrists. What is the sound of a forgotten word? What do we do when all we can remember is the taste of the smoke?

***

pressing flowers

i wake up in
this weeping wound
of a world and wonder

if today will
finally slit the throat
of time in two

before
                    after

or if we will
lap up its blood
and forget

(the everyday violence of living)

in grief, i
gather these
bruised-petal days

and tuck them
between two sheets,
for safekeeping.

***

As I tried to archive a messy and desperately sad present, I turned to how our lives were captured in the past. At a time of mass disablement and death, I wanted to see some trace of life. But time and time again, the archive brought me back to death. In Alison Wong's novel *As the*

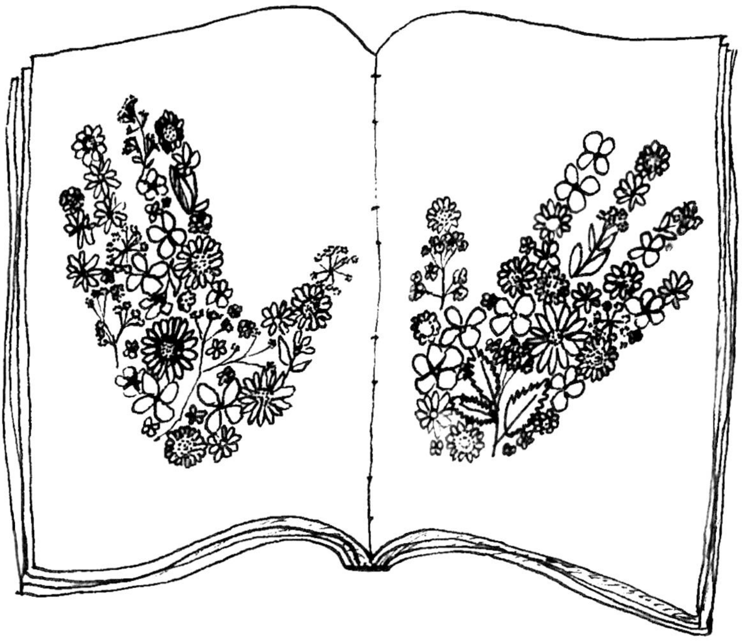

Figure 9.2 *Pressing Flowers*, by Lucy Smith, 2024. *Source*: © Lucy Smith 2024.

Earth Turns Silver (2015), a widowed Pākehā[1] New Zealand woman, Katherine, falls in love with a kind and gracious Chinese grocery shop owner, Yung. I read the novel during the COVID-19 lockdown, hoping for a momentary release from the never-ending anxiety of those pandemic ridden days. But as the two embarked on their inevitably doomed love affair, I found my own ability to care was stifled. *I could not care for them*. For I knew that there was no end to this love story other than death, and specifically, Yung's death, the death of the Chinese man.

The novel foreshadows Yung's death with the historically accurate account of the murder of Joe Kum Yung, an elderly Chinese gold miner. In 1905, he was shot on Wellington's Haining Street by the White supremacist Lionel Terry, for no other reason but to prove that the death of a Chinese man at his hands was not defensible as murder, the unlawful killing of another human being. Terry was a disillusioned White supremacist writer, poet and activist, who wanted to purge the British Empire of 'alien races'. One Sunday night, Terry went hunting for

[1] Māori term for a white New Zealander, usually of European descent.

a Chinese man – any Chinese man – to prove that Chinese people were not human under the law. The day after he shot Joe Kum Yung, Terry turned himself in to the New Zealand authorities, with the belief that he could – and should – win his legal case.

Joe Kum Yung's death haunted that novel, and it continued to haunt me. The more I looked for traces of his life and death in the archives, the more he eluded me. This is all I could find out about Joe Kum Yung: he was a miner from Guangdong; his leg was badly damaged in a mining accident; he became destitute; he was killed by a White supremacist. Joe Kum Yung would not have made any trace on the books of history were he not murdered by Terry. His life is only visible to me in the event of his violation, the cruel moment of his disappearance.

Lionel Terry is his exact opposite. Unlike Joe Kum Yung, he *lives*. At the trial, Terry is sentenced to death, but the sentence was commuted on the basis of his evident insanity. He spends the rest of his life sectioned in mental hospitals. He is also unlike Joe Kum Yung in that he emerges, time and time again, in the historical record. Unlike Yung, who is portrayed as elderly, crippled and destitute, Terry is described as tall and handsome, even heroic. Courtroom illustrations portray Terry as statuesque, with a Roman nose and an upright posture (Figure 9.3). The Chinese witnesses

Figure 9.3 Courtroom illustrations: *The Lionel Terry Murder Trial*, by E. F. Hiscocks. *Source*: *Auckland Weekly News*, 1905.

and onlookers, in contrast, are drawn through the lens of Mirzoeff's 'White sight': shrivelled and shrunken, speaking with twisted tongues in a cruel mockery of their accents.

Terry becomes a figure of public fascination, even hero worship. As Brian Moloughney and John Stenhouse note: 'when Terry escaped from Sunnyside and Seacliff hospitals into the South Island countryside, as he did for weeks at a time, sympathizers hailed him as a people's hero, and helped him evade capture' (Moloughney and Stenhouse 1999, 43–4). His White supremacist tract, *The Shadow*, was republished in 1984 by the neo-fascist group the New Zealand Nationalist Workers Party (Terry 1984). The timing of *The Shadow*'s re-emergence is hardly surprising. New Zealand, in the 1980s, experienced heightened levels of anti-Chinese prejudice and violence in response to Asian immigration: the so-called 'Asian invasion'. In 2020, a national New Zealand high school history exam paper even featured one of Terry's poems as an example for students to write about and analyse.

As Chris Tse writes in his poetry collection, about Joe Kum Yung's life and death, *How to be Dead in a Year of Snakes:*

Lionel's legacy in the history books:
racist, murderer.
But where is Joe?

Ah –
    he's with Lionel. (Tse 2014, 63)

Mapped against the death of Joe Kum Yung, the other, even less remarked-upon murders of Chinese migrants and labourers, the slew of anti-Chinese immigration laws that laid a stiff £10 tax on every head, that permitted only one Chinese human to enter the country per hundred tons of cargo, is it surprising that I could not bring myself to care for Katherine and Yung's doomed love affair? How could I care for them when 'one Sunday, Lionel Terry went hunting for a Chinaman' (Tse 2014, 19)?

***

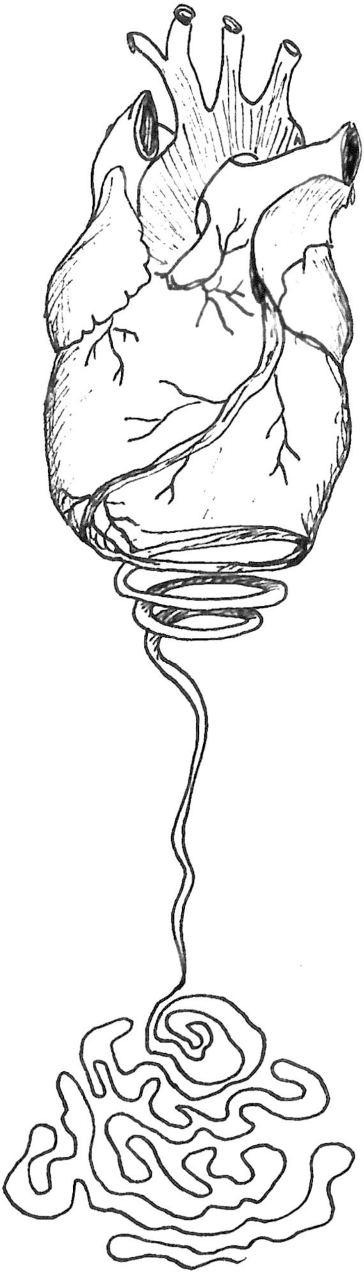

Figure 9.4 *Compassion Fatigue*, by Lucy Smith, 2024. *Source*: © Lucy Smith 2024.

compassion fatigue

today, my heart is an overtired
child, wailing, inconsolable;

she won't be quietened
with sweets and promises that everything

will be fine; she has the wisdom
of a child, which is to say, no wisdom,

which is to say, no false pretensions,
like knowing you did everything right

so here she is, my heart, a gagging,
snot-slick, opera of grief. my heart

is ill-behaved, badly-trained, a
natural consequence of letting it roam

too freely; and everyone who sees
this dreadful, shrieking scene is simply

glad it is not theirs. what i am trying
to say is that my heart is spoilt,

excessive; but how does one pare back
a heart? is it like peeling the skin from

an apple? whittled away in a gleaming spiral,
coiled around the blade of the knife?

is that why justice tore out her eyes?
did even her tears have to apologise?

finally, she quietens, my wrung-out
heart, all worn like the blanket clasped

in one hand and the dirty feather she
found in the other. soft, she had said,

and held it against my face. soft,
i had said, and tucked her head into the

space between my neck and shoulder
blade. soft, i say, and let her rest.

***

I am on a sunny holiday with my family in New Zealand when we are struck by a summer storm. When rain falls on hot concrete, it produces a peculiar smell. It is hot and warm: the prick of a tear behind an eyelid. My mother remarks that it reminds her of Suva, of being a kid growing up in Fiji. Perhaps one day there will be an archive that can capture my mother's childhood memories of Suva: the smell of rain on hot concrete.

In her essay, 'Venus in two acts', Saidiya Hartman posits, 'it is an impossible writing which attempts to say that which resists being said (since dead girls are unable to speak). It is a history of an unrecoverable past; it is a narrative of what might have been or could have been; it is a history written with and against the archive' (Hartman 2008, 12). Hartman emphasises the need for narrative restraint, to tell an impossible story by amplifying the impossibility of its telling. Her method of critical fabulation strains against the limits of the archive, reading both with and against the grain, in order to 'to reckon with the precarious lives which are visible only in the moment of their disappearance'. Hartman's historical method reminds me of how my gung gung (maternal grandfather) taught me to slice meat: across, rather than along, the grain, so that it would be tender. When I next return to an archive, I hope, somehow, that I will find tenderness nestled between those sheets.

In the meantime, I turn to Chris Tse's poetry as a counter-archival project, as an artistic work of critical fabulation that attempts to find glimpses of our violently forgotten lives percolating amid the earthy grounds of death. Tse strains against the limits of the archive and Yung's appearance only in his very moment of disappearance: 'So there goes a life story reduced / to one gunshot / and there goes madness / in the form of public service / and there wait those graceless thieves / of light and sound / slipping to a snake's crawl / to rewrite his truths' (Tse 2014, 42). Yet, his poetry creates an aperture for imagining Yung's archival death and life differently. As Tse concludes: 'even if his name still hooks to yours / there will be voices to say your name / to clear the way. The rest is up to you' (Tse 2014, 69).

So I turn to a different, no less impossible archive: an archive of tears, of souls turned into steam, of water becoming memory. Toni

Morrison says that all water has a perfect memory and is forever trying to get back to where it was (Morrison 1995). I feel guilty for loving the ocean when I think of all the lives it has taken. But I am land-sick, and the sea cannot be stolen. I map my body and my history through the complex tides of love and hate. I think of the undercurrents that bring my family together and push us apart. I smell rain on hot concrete and revel in the excess beating within me, the simultaneity of the sun and the storm. I pour myself and my liquid excess into the vessel of the archive. It starts to leak. The archive tries to contain me, but I turn it into a vessel of my own. I use this ship to cross its borders. I know, given its way, the archive would grind me down into knucklebones. But I make the archive shatter; it will not shatter me. I am not bound by its categories.

For once, I am not the one falling apart.

References

Butler, Judith. 2003. 'Violence, mourning, politics', *Studies in Gender and Sexuality* 4(1): 9–37. https://doi.org/10.1080/15240650409349213.

Deleuze, Gilles, Félix Guattari and Brian Massumi. 2004. *A Thousand Plateaus: Capitalism and schizophrenia*. London: Continuum.

Ellmann, Maud. 1993. *The Hunger Artists: Starving, writing and imprisonment*. Cambridge, MA: Harvard University Press.

Hartman, Saidiya. 2008. 'Venus in two acts', *Small Axe: A journal of criticism* 12(2): 1–14. https://doi.org/10.1215/-12-2-1.

Hiscocks, E. F. 1905. 'The Lionel Terry murder trial', *Auckland Weekly News*. Accessed 26 January 2024. https://digitalnz.org/records/29962972.

Kristeva, Julia. 1982. *Powers of Horror: An essay on abjection*. New York: Columbia University Press.

Mirzoeff, Nicholas. 2023. *White Sight: Visual politics and practices of whiteness*. Cambridge, MA: MIT Press.

Moloughney, Brian and John Stenhouse. 1999. '"Drug-besotten sin-begotten fiends of filth": New Zealanders and the Oriental other, 1850–1920', *New Zealand Journal of History* 33(1). Accessed 26 January 2024. https://muse.jhu.edu/article/874262.

Morrison, Toni. 1995. 'The site of memory'. In *Inventing the Truth: The art and craft of memoir*, 2nd edition, edited by William Zinsser, 83–102. Boston: Houghton Mifflin.

Royal, Te Ahukaramū Charles. 2007. 'Papatūānuku: the land. Whenua: the placenta', *Te Ara: The Encyclopedia of New Zealand*. Accessed 27 January 2024. https://www.TeAra.govt.nz/en/papatuanuku-the-land/page-4.

Terry, Lionel. 1984. *The Shadow*. Lower Hutt, Wellington: Nationalist Workers Party.

Tse, Chris. 2014. *How to be Dead in a Year of Snakes*. Auckland: Auckland University Press.

Wong, Alison. 2015. *As the Earth Turns Silver*. Auckland: Pan Macmillan.

Index

Page numbers followed by 'n' refer to information in notes.